Joseph and Aseneth

Guides to Apocrypha and Pseudepigrapha

Series Editor

Michael A. Knibb

JOSEPH AND ASENETH

Edith M. Humphrey

Sheffield
Academic Press

Copyright © 2000 Sheffield Academic Press

Published by Sheffield Academic Press Ltd
Mansion House
19 Kingfield Road
Sheffield S11 9AS
England

Printed on acid-free paper in Great Britain
by The Cromwell Press
Trowbridge, Wiltshire

British Library Cataloguing in Publication Data

A catalogue record for this book is available
from the British Library

ISBN 1-84127-083-0

Contents

Preface

'Of making many books there is no end.' Never has this saying seemed more appropriate than during my renewed study of *Aseneth* and the secondary literature associated with her name. The past decade, and in particular the past four years, have seen an explosion of scholarly discussion concerning this tiny and heretofore obscure apocryphon—an explosion seemingly out of proportion to *Aseneth*'s size and literary mode. How is it that a popular work from two millennia ago, undignified even by canonical status, is receiving such attention?

No doubt the major reason is the tantalizing puzzle that this book presents. In resuming my study of *Aseneth* after several years, I have been entranced yet again by the apocryphon; I have also been pleased to discover how this short ancient work provides an apt window into the complexities of contemporary scholarship in the postmodern age. Students may well take *Aseneth* as a test case in their approach to scholarly method, and to the varied realm of ancient literature. Chapters 2 and 3 of this volume treat these two areas, offering first an introduction to the major issues and debates that have surrounded *Aseneth*, and next an interpretation of the piece itself. The hybrid approach that I adopt in Chapter 3 (rhetorical-literary) is intended to respond both to the demands of a deceptively 'simple' text and to the many-layered questions that are being asked of texts today. It is offered as one way of reading *Aseneth*, and will, I hope, inspire others to enter into the intriguing world of this long-lived text.

Thanks are especially due to those who engaged me in important ways during the preparation of this manuscript—to Michael Knibb, Nathalie Polzer, Gideon Bohak, Ross S. Kraemer, Fiona Black, Randall Chesnutt, and my husband Chris. I am also profoundly grateful to the members of the Canadian Society of Biblical Studies who tolerated a hypostasized presentation of *Aseneth* while I was in the throes of research, and to my daughter Joëlle, who delighted me with her response to the story one stormy summer afternoon. To Joëlle and Alexandra, who put ashes in their hair, and to Meredith, who has promised to name her first-born daughter Aseneth, I dedicate this study.

Primary Sources and Translations

Batiffol, P., *Le livre de la prière d'Aséneth* (Studia Patristica: Études d'ancienne littérature chrétienne, 1-2; Paris: Leroux, 1889–90). The first full publication of a Greek text (based on family *a*), coupled with an edition of a Latin version (manuscripts provided by M.R. James).

Brooks, E.W., *Joseph and Asenath* (TED, 2; London: SPCK, 1918). Brooks's English translation follows Batiffol's Greek text, based on family *a*, and is therefore of limited value.

Burchard, C., 'Joseph and Aseneth', in J.H. Charlesworth (ed.), *The Old Testament Pseudepigrapha*, II (2 vols.; Garden City, NY: Doubleday, 1983–85), pp. 177-247. An English translation of his own eclectic text, with introduction and notes.

—'Ein vorläufiger griechischer Text von *Joseph und Aseneth*', *DBAT* 14 (1979), pp. 2-53 is completed by his 'Verbesserungen zum vorläufigen Text von Joseph und Aseneth', *DBAT* 16 (1982), pp. 37-39. These two works provide Burchards's reconstructed eclectic text, leaning on family *b*. The text is presented here without accents or aspiration.

Cook, D., 'Joseph and Aseneth', in H.F.D. Sparks (ed.), *The Apocryphal Old Testament* (Oxford: Clarendon Press, 1984), pp. 465-503. Cook's English translation follows Philonenko's shorter Greek text, based on family *d*.

Denis, A.-M., OP, *Concordance grecque des pseudépigraphes d'Ancien Testament: Concordance, corpus des textes, indices*. Avec la collaboration d'Yvonne Janssens et le concours du CETEDOC (Louvain-la-Neuve: Université Catholique de Louvain, 1987), pp. 851-59. Denis reproduces Burchard's provisional text, adding aspiration and accents.

Kraemer, Ross S., *Maenads, Martyrs, Matrons, Monastics: A Sourcebook on Women's Religions in the Greco-Roman World* (Philadelphia: Fortress Press, 1988), pp. 263-79. Kraemer's English contemporary translation (like that of Cook) is based on Philonenko's text, but includes only chs. 1–21.

Philonenko, Marc, *Joseph et Aséneth: Introduction, texte critique, traduction et notes* (SPB, 13; Leiden: E.J. Brill, 1968). Philonenko's Greek text and French translation are based on family *d*.

Abbreviations

ABD	David Noel Freedman (ed.), *The Anchor Bible Dictionary* (New York: Doubleday, 1992)
AGJU	Arbeiten zur Geschichte des antiken Judentums und des Urchristentums
ANRW	Hildegard Temporini and Wolfgang Haase (eds.), *Aufstieg und Niedergang der römischen Welt: Geschichte und Kultur Roms im Spiegel der neueren Forschung* (Berlin: W. de Gruyter, 1972–)
ARC	The Journal of the Faculty of Religious Studies, McGill University, Montreál, Canada
BJS	*Brown Judaic Studies*
BLE	*Bulletin de littérature ecclésiastique*
CETEDOC	Centre de Traitement Electroniques des Documents, Louvain-la Neuve
CQR	*Classical Quarterly Review*
DBAT	*Dielheimer Blätter zum Alten Testament*
DJD	Discoveries in the Judaean Desert
EncJud	*Encyclopaedia Judaica*
ExpTim	*Expository Times*
HSS	*Harvard Semitic Studies*
JBL	*Journal of Biblical Literature*
JewEnc	*The Jewish Encyclopedia*
JSJ	*Journal for the Study of Judaism*
JSNT	*Journal for the Study of the New Testament*
JSP	*Journal for the Study of the Pseudepigrapha*
JSPSup	*Journal for the Study of the Pseudepigrapha*, Supplement Series
JSOTSup	*Journal for the Study of the Old Testament*, Supplement Series
NLH	*New Literary History*
NTS	*New Testament Studies*
OTP	*Old Testament Pseudepigrapha*
RB	*Revue biblique*

RechBib	*Recherches bibliques*
SBL	Society of Biblical Literature
SPB	*Studia postbiblica*
SBLSP	*SBL Seminar Papers*
TED	Translations of Early Documents
TQ	*Theologische Quartalschrift*
WUNT	Wissenschaftliche Untersuchungen zum Neuen Testament
ZNW	*Zeitschrift für die neutestamentliche Wissenschaft*

1

INTRODUCTION

Once upon a time—to be more (or less) precise, during the sojourn of
the Hebrews in Egypt—there was a girl who, like all self-respecting
heroines, possessed superlative height, beauty and virtue. Her name was
Aseneth (Asen*ath* in the Hebrew text of Gen. 41.45, 50; 46.20), and
she lived with her mother and priestly father Pentephres (Potiphera) in
the city of Heliopolis (On). Although Aseneth shared in the beauty of
the Hebrew women, she was, with the rest of her family, a Gentile.
This posed a serious problem, since, according to the records of the
Almighty (as we subsequently discover), she had been designated the
bride of the patriarch Joseph from eternity. Her virtue and pride, however, stood her in good stead, for she repeatedly rebuffed the advances
of her numerous suitors (even Pharaoh's son!) and remained in purity
with seven waiting-virgins in the tower-room chambers adjacent to her
father's house, far from the eye of even a male child. It seems her father
did not consider her pedigree to be an insuperable obstacle, for he rec-
ommended Joseph to his daughter as a suitable husband. The suggestion was, not surprisingly, met by Aseneth's characteristic disdain of
men—particularly of this one, who, according to rumour, had been
intimate with someone else's wife!

And so Joseph comes calling, on his quest of gathering grain against
the seven years of famine to come (Gen. 41.46-49). He is ceremoniously greeted by the Heliopolitan priest, who considerately sets out for
him a separate table. Aseneth, in glimpsing this illustrious, almost
angelic visitor, is overwhelmed, and comes to greet him. But the tables
of aloofness have been turned. Joseph will not salute her: her mouth is
unclean through the blessing of foreign gods. Instead, he prays for her,
conferring a three-fold blessing, and goes on his way, with a promise to

return on the eighth day. In utter dismay, Aseneth withdraws to her chamber, alone, fasting and praying for a week, dressing in black and repenting of her idolatry and pride. The morning star of the eighth day heralds a celestial Visitor who appears as the epitome of Joseph himself, only more glorious. This unnamed chief messenger of God comes to Aseneth to fulfil and confirm Joseph's earlier blessing. After encouraging her with comforting words, he sends her to wash and exchange her mourning garb for something more radiant, telling her that a veil of modesty is unnecessary. He declares her acceptance, tells her of the mediation of God's heavenly daughter Repentance, and confers on her the name 'City of Refuge'. Finally, he feeds her with a mysterious honeycomb, which he interprets as heavenly food, drink and unction. The blessings are capped by a mysterious revelation: the honeycomb is marked by his finger in a curious manner and exotic bees swarm from it to be with Aseneth, acting in various ways (depending on which version of the story one is reading). Although the Visitor never divulges his name, he departs after promising that she will indeed be Joseph's bride. Remembering the heavenly messenger's command, Aseneth dresses as a bride, and in seeing the reflection of her face, is amazed to see that she has been gloriously transformed. The difference is evident to all, including Joseph, who arrives after having received a twin (but offstage) vision informing him of her conversion. The two are married by Pharaoh himself, and Aseneth gives birth to Manasseh and Ephraim, the fathers of the half-tribes.

And so they live happily ever after. But not quite yet: action follows! Pharaoh's son plots against his own father and Joseph, aiming to take Aseneth for himself. He ambushes Aseneth, aided by the sons of Bilhah and Zilpah, especially Gad and Dan. He is, however, opposed by Joseph's brothers: Levi, who has prophetic powers, and Benjamin, who carries himself like a young David, play particularly heroic roles. At the height of the action, Aseneth utters a prayer of hope and is saved by divine intervention. Pharaoh's son is wounded, and the two treacherous brothers beg forgiveness, which is bountifully given by Aseneth the merciful. Pharaoh's son, however, dies, followed by his broken-hearted father, and so Joseph is left regent of all Egypt, acting as guardian of Pharaoh's infant son until he comes of age.

These twin narratives, the first treating Aseneth's conversion, enlightenment and marriage, and the second offering an adventure, have fired the imaginations of not a few generations and communities, as is clear from the numerous versions and languages in which the story has been told. Like other parabiblical 'novels', *Joseph and Aseneth* (or *Aseneth*, as we shall call it) answers to the perennial desire of the wayward reader to 'fill in the blanks' or write 'between the lines' of the biblical narrative; yet, its parabiblical and mystic style afford it, in its turn, a polyvalence. *Aseneth* itself does not tie up all the loose ends, but leaves its own *aporiai* to beguile and entrance readers of various backgrounds. Moreover, the book hovers on the edge of generic categories, blending styles that are frequently seen in 'purer' forms. As a romance, it has a popular appeal; as a parabiblical book with intertextual echoes, it speaks poignantly to the biblically literate; as a piece with an extended revelatory section, and with portions heavily influenced by sapiential and mystical traditions, it intrigues yet others. This unique combination of traditions, conventions and themes is greater than the sum of the parts, so that repeated readings of *Aseneth* will yield new surprises and new hermeneutical possibilities. No doubt for those who have already more than a nodding acquaintance with the book, the epitome of the plot given above has disappointed in one or other particular: some favourite scene, symbolic network or intertextual connection has been, of necessity, omitted. The richness of allusion and generic play in the piece render it irreducible: it can be contained neither by a synopsis nor a statement of purpose, but must be travelled through and enjoyed in full.

Given the potential for engagement at so many various levels, it is lamentable that *Aseneth* is no longer read on a popular level. With the exception of those in the Eastern Christian tradition (who know her from the Orthodox wedding liturgy) even the name of Aseneth remains obscure enough to be an elite 'trivia' question. This was not always the case. While the tracing of the tale's career is fraught with difficulties, clearly Aseneth's story enjoyed considerable fame in antiquity and was told, with variation, in both Jewish and Christian circles. It is also certain that in the Christian East, particularly in Armenia, the story remained in vibrant connection with the culture: some Armenian Bibles even include *Aseneth* among their apocryphal additions, along with illustrations of the couple. In the West, the story experienced a revival of popularity in the mid-thirteenth century, due partly to a short Latin rendering of the tale in the *Speculum historiale* (1.118-124) of Vincent de Beauvais. *Aseneth* thus appears in several versions and European languages, as well as other Latin renderings, during the Middle Ages up to 1745, when an Icelandic text was published. In England the story was popular enough to be enshrined in Middle

English verse and in a sixteenth-century Corpus Christi play. From the East, we also have extant texts and manuscript fragments in Syriac, Serbian Slavonic, Romanian, Ethiopian and Armenian, most of uncertain dating, and based upon earlier texts of uncertain dating, which came to light in the eighteenth and nineteenth centuries. No doubt the ascendancy of Protestant Christianity, with its emphasis on *sola scriptura*, had a dimming effect on the memory of the West; after the baroque period the story gradually lost its hold on the popular imagination. However, the name has continued to be used especially in Armenian and English circles, although sporadically. Burchard, in his introduction to the book in *The Old Testament Pseudepigrapha*, II ([ed. J.H. Charlesworth; 2 vols.; Garden City, NY: Doubleday, 1985], pp. 177-201) cites seventeenth- and eighteenth-century English occurrences of the name, and then suggests that this usage has died: he would be surprised to know that the present writer is distinguished by having an Irish second cousin with the name Aseneth!

The generic and allusive complexity of the book, coupled with its rich history of transmission, has ensured that the secondary literature associated with *Aseneth* is both proliferous and multi-directioned. To read *Aseneth* is to be intrigued by a deceptively simple text; to read the secondary literature to begin an hydra-like quest of text-type, genre, symbology, *Sitz im Leben*, purpose, sociological analysis, ideological concerns and appropriate method. Recent encyclopaedia articles, and Burchard's standard introduction in Charlesworth's *OTP* give the impression of a new scholarly consensus, which was probably a reasonable hope in the 1980s. At the time, it looked to many as though the dating, provenance, nature and purpose of *Aseneth* had been settled, within certain parameters. The nineteenth-century scholar Batiffol, who prematurely categorized the book as Byzantine, had been refuted, and Burchard's careful championing of the longer text-type, accompanied by an exciting new eclectic text, translated into English, seemed bound to win the day. Scholars had in general heeded warnings against the extremes of mirror-reading and 'parallelomania' and were much more cautious in tying texts to other texts, or to specific social groups; in the case of *Aseneth*, attempts to find a link with Christian practices, such as the Eucharist and chrismation, or with particular cults (such as that of the Therapeutae) found between the lines of the text, were no longer fashionable. The emerging 'consensus' was that *Aseneth* was written by a Hellenistic Jewish writer, between aproximately 100 BCE and 115 CE, to those concerned with the status of proselytes in a relatively mainstream Hellenistic Jewish community, probably located in Egypt.

But simplicity was not to be *Aseneth*'s happy fate. Challenges concerning the dating, nature, text-type and provenance of the book again have been launched, and it must be admitted that the scholarly consensus was too optimistically announced. A new dimension to the critical conversation has shifted the debate: no longer are we simply to search for the best solutions to earlier questions, but must ask *which* are the appropriate questions to pose. For example, it was assumed until recently that scholars needed to determine the text or textual family that most closely corresponded to the elusive *Ur*-text of a work; a text, or at least a provisional text needed to be established as a prior task to analysis. In the postmodern atmosphere, however, arguments are being made for the fruitful study of *all* the possible variations, so as to give a thicker understanding of the story's reflection of, or influence upon various communities, and so as to open up a multitude of interpretative possibilities for today. The question is not necessarily which is the earliest and 'best' text, but rather how this and/or that text is implicated in the questions and stories of a past generation and of today.

The student of *Aseneth* is presented with two worlds: the engaging yet complex world of the story itself, and an ongoing conversation that participates in the ambiguities of biblical scholarship today. This apocryphon is in fact illustrative of the many specific questions that arise in the analysis of ancient literature, and its study will provide an *entrée* into foundational issues. In the following pages, we will consider each of the areas of debate, beginning with the problem of the text itself; these explorations will be followed by a rhetorical-literary reading of *Aseneth* that seeks to do justice to its narratival and revelatory nature. Finally, a voice will be given to *Aseneth*, who pleads for her integrity, while confronted by the spectre of disagreeing specialists. It is hoped that this final word will remind the reader that secondary material is not primary, and that guides are simply guides: the world of the text stands before us to enter, explore and enjoy.

Further Reading

Encyclopaedia and General Articles on Aseneth

Burchard, C.,'Joseph and Aseneth', in J.H. Charlesworth (ed.), *The Old Testament Pseudepigrapha*, II (2 vols.; Garden City, NY: Doubleday, 1983–85), pp. 177-247. Thorough brief introduction and translation with notes by an eminent scholar.

Chesnutt, R.D., 'Joseph and Aseneth', in D.N. Freedman (ed.), *Anchor Bible Dictionary*, III (6 vols.; New York: Doubleday, 1992), pp. 969-71. A helpful article representing the 'consensus' of the last decade.

Kohler, K., 'Asenath, Life and Confession or Prayer of', *JewEnc*, II (1902), pp. 172-76. An early article arguing for Jewish character, connection with the Essenes, minimal Christian interpolations, and missionary impulse.

Kraemer, Ross, 'The Book of Aseneth', in E. Schüssler Fiorenza, *Searching the Scriptures: A Feminist Commentary*, II (Atlanta, GA: Scholars Press, 1994), pp. 787-816. Concise representation of Kraemer's developing views on the apocryphon.

Philonenko, M. 'Joseph and Asenath', *EncJud*, X, cols. 223-24. A distillation of Philonenko's views in English.

O'Neil, J.C., 'What Is Joseph and Aseneth About?', *Henoch* 16 (1994), pp. 189-98. A reading and introduction to the apocryphon including source-critical theory and analysis.

On the Textual Traditions of Aseneth

Burchard, C., *Untersuchungen zu Joseph und Aseneth: Überlieferung-Ortsbestimmung* (WUNT, 8; Tübingen: J.C.B. Mohr [Paul Siebeck], 1965). Burchard's influential monograph includes a comprehensive first section on the textual traditions. For an epitome of his arguments in English, see his introduction in *OTP*, II, pp. 178-81.

Philonenko, Marc, *Joseph et Aséneth: Introduction, texte critique, traduction et notes* (SPB, 13; Leiden: E.J. Brill, 1968). Philonenko's study of the textual tradition is found mainly in the introduction, but also represented in the notes to the critical text.

On Methodological Pluralism

Barton, John, *Reading the Old Testament: Method in Biblical Study* (Louisville, KY: Westminster/John Knox Press, 1984 and 1996). Barton's analysis and critique of multiple methods used in the study of the Old Testament are also helpful for the study of Aseneth.

Kraemer, Ross S., *When Aseneth Met Joseph: A Late Antique Tale of the Biblical Patriarch and his Egyptian Wife, Reconsidered* (New York: Oxford University Press, 1998). See especially Kraemer's introductory remarks on 'textual dilemmas' and 'genre', pp. 6-12.

2

ISSUES IN READING AND INTERPRETATION

1. Which Family? Which Text?

We begin with questions that are often considered to be preliminary, though not elementary, in the study of a text. Quite frequently, analysts presuppose the decisions of specialists in 'lower criticism' (which establishes the text itself) in order to get on with their task, whatever that may be. This is possible when there is broad agreement concerning superior text-type(s), as in the New Testament, but not in *Aseneth*. Although the textual history of *Aseneth* is rather complicated for the non-specialist, students may not at present consider the issue settled and glibly move on to 'higher' or 'deeper' matters. Rather, the textual traditions and arguments for certain texts need to be understood because of the conflicting opinions that are being currently articulated. In fact, the textual problems are integrally connected with other issues, as decisions about text-types increasingly are being made not simply on the basis of traditional text-critical methods, but by reference to *contextual* questions such as *cui bono?* (i.e. to whom, to which community, would this be helpful?) That is, it is urged that we consider the differences, and (where these can be determined) the overall tendencies of the various versions, and seek theological or sociological reasons for these, thus proposing possible scenarios of textual development. It is therefore not surprising that the pattern of scholarship followed in the textual area mirrors the problem of *Sitz im Leben* discussed briefly in the introduction: first, chaotic and varied analyses; second, tomes from major scholars who championed different views; third, the seeming emergence of a consensus; and finally, the breakdown of that agreement in recent years. Do we need even to establish the text that lies closest to an *Ur*-text, or is it more valuable to appreciate the various versions for their different contributions?

Burchard's Long or Philonenko's Short Text?

Let us plunge in at the second stage (major studies after a period of chaos) and consider the writings of two influential and opposing scholars: a monograph by C. Burchard in 1965 (*Untersuchungen zu Joseph und Aseneth* [WUNT, 8; Tübingen: J.C.B. Mohr [Paul Siebeck]), another by Marc Philonenko in 1968 (*Joseph et Aséneth: Introduction, texte critique, traduction et notes* [SPB, 13; Leiden: E.J. Brill]). Their independent analyses of the 16 Greek manuscripts of *Aseneth* led them to concur in one particular: that the texts could be divided into (at least) four distinct groups, or families, labelled *a*, *b*, *c*, and *d*. Simple observation showed *a* and *b* to be longer than the other two; P. Batiffol's earlier work (*Le livre de la prière d'Aséneth* [Studia Patristica, 1; Paris: Leroux, 1889], pp. 1-115) had established a text based on the longest *a* family, which both Burchard and Philonenko rejected as too polished for an 'original'. Family *c* was not a serious candidate for originality on similar stylistic grounds, and because it is incomplete.

Here all agreement ended. Philonenko was convinced that he had found the oldest text family *d*, the shortest form. Thus he constructed his preferred text on the basis of two *d* manuscripts, with reference to a linked Slavonic version; only at a few points did he add passages from the longer recensions, where it seemed clear they had been omitted by *d* texts. In contrast, Burchard saw family *b* as superior, and began work towards a new eclectic edition based on several *b* manuscripts, but with reference to other families where necessary, and in full awareness of the Latin, Syriac and Armenian versions that are related to *b*. So then, Philonenko considered that the lost *Ur*-text is most closely represented by the short texts in family *d*: this text had been expanded variously in the two longer text-types *a* and *b*. Burchard, on the other hand, argued for the priority of a longer text, represented best by family *b*, and saw the short text-types as abbreviations.

What difference does it make to give priority to one text or the other? First, if Philonenko's short recension *d* is accepted, then several significant blocks of material are to be seen as later redaction, including parts of the central revelatory section, and the 'Psalm of Aseneth' (21.10-21) that closes Part One. There are also interesting differences with regard to the language used for the heavenly figure Metanoia ('Repentance', 'Penitence', 'Conversion', 15.7), the language used for God and the perspective from which Aseneth is described: these variations are important especially for feminist analyses of the book. It seems, however, as though Burchard's text has been and will continue to be favoured by most scholars. This may be partly a result of its translation in Charlesworth's *OTP*; it may also be partially by default, since Philonenko quit the debate in the 1970s and there has been no subsequent technical defence of his text.

Kraemer: Inductive Arguments for the Short Text and Later Dating

Most recently, Ross Kraemer has argued that the shorter text is probably earlier than *b*, although she distances herself from any attempt to establish an original version on the grounds that such a search is 'inextricably' connected with theological preconceptions (Ross Shepard Kraemer, *When Aseneth Met Joseph: A Late Antique Tale of the Biblical Patriarch and his Egyptian Wife, Reconsidered* [New York: Oxford University Press, 1998], p. 305). Instead of a technical text-critical analysis, she presents a cumulative case, comparing the content of the two major recensions in connection with parallels from late antiquity and questions of provenance and dating. This issues in a conviction that *b* is mainly an intentional revision of an earlier form approximated by Philonenko's *d* (although Burchard's text may sometimes preserve early material deleted from *d*).

By adopting a wholly inductive approach, Kraemer's case for the earlier recension is arguably weakened. We are told in the introduction that she has been convinced through her own painstaking comparison of texts, and then are invited to follow her reasoning as she analyses first the short text, then what she considers to be the 'recomposed' longer text. In her view, the longer text shows evidence of careful rewriting, engaging in more explicit biblical imagery and the smoothing of ambiguities. Throughout her reading, Kraemer proposes questions that may have bothered earliest readers of the short text, and answers that are supposedly furnished by the longer redacted version. Some of these questions are odd, however, and the answers given present more problems than they solve. For example, would the reader of a *romance* ask, at the point where the lovers are finally united, 'what prompted Joseph to kiss Aseneth's hand…and which hand did she kiss' (*When Aseneth*, p. 76)? Puzzlement rather than enlightenment is the natural response to *b*'s mystical reference to Aseneth's 'right' hand which is 'like that of a fast-writing scribe' (20.5). This is singularly odd language for a love story! Although such decisions involve an element of judgment, it seems much more likely that a redactor has omitted these strange details than that they have been added for supposed clarification.

Many other details interpreted by Kraemer to establish an earlier short text may be read differently. She argues that *b*'s specification of 'which bees' in the honeycomb episode is an editorial clarification: however, the division of bees into two camps, and details of what happens to each (16.20-23), adds mystery to the revelatory narrative, prompting a series of new questions. Again, she sees the longer text as correcting the statement that Pharaoh is 'Joseph's father' by adding the qualifier '*like* Joseph's father' (20.9)—but this could represent a careless omission by *d* in the second place, rather than a correction by *b* of an earlier gaffe by *d*. On the other hand, the shorter text may be observed to add a reference to the devil (12.10 in Philonenko's edition), and to embellish upon the leonine imagery found in both versions (12.9-10 in Burchard; 12.9 in Philonenko) by describing Aseneth's enemy as a wolf (uniquely in 12.10, Philonenko's text). These modifications within Aseneth's plea for protection do in fact read like a clarification or theological exposition of the longer text's more ambiguous imagery (12.10-11 in Burchard versus 12.9-10 in Philonenko). Kraemer also suggests that the sequence of the divine calling of Aseneth in the short text (a single call followed by a double call at 14.4-6) is modelled on a Hebrew text of such passages as Gen. 22.1, 22.11 and 1 Kgs 3.4—or on a Greek translation closer to the Hebrew text than the Septuagint. (The Septuagint or a similar version informs the longer text.) She neglects to notice, however, that the custom is not consistent even in the Hebrew text (see Gen. 46.2; Exod. 3.4, where there is simply a double call). Again, Kraemer assumes that the heavenly Visitor's third person speech regarding God's acceptance of Aseneth (15.2 in the short text) is natural, and that it has been changed to the first person by a redactor in the longer text. Is it not more likely that a redactor found first person language in the mouth of a subordinate troublesome and so modified the longer version? Nor are the cited 'corrections' entirely consistent—at one point Kraemer states that the longer text obscures the connection between Aseneth and male role models (*When Aseneth*, p. 51); at another point she calls attention to marked similarities in the longer text between Aseneth, Manoah and Jacob (*When Aseneth*, p. 63)! At one point, an added episode (18.2-5 in Burchard) is said to minimize the impact of Aseneth's 'angelic' transformation; yet it must be admitted that the longer version emphasizes this transformation repeatedly, as character after character is amazed by her glory. Other examples could be given.

Central to Kraemer's view is the strong concern of the longer text for the 'Name-bearing angel' and an imputed closer connection with later mystical texts. Even the shorter version is replete with details common to third- and fourth-century writings—the adjuration of angels, transformation of the visionary, Neo-Platonic concepts of the soul, and the like. However, she argues that the longer exemplifies a greater affinity with merkavah mysticism, that is, rabbinic 'chariot' mysticism that included explicit preparation, meditation and esoteric experiences. (See section 4 of this chapter for a closer discussion of these issues.) The discovery of similarities here is not in itself determinative of a late date for either text-type, however. While explicit merkavah mysticism is clearly attested only in later antiquity, many researchers have noted the presence of analogous understandings and practices in various groups long before the third century CE. (Kraemer suggests that the most recent studies argue that merkavah materials had a late origin [*When Aseneth*, p. 106 n. 8.] While this is so, a range of opinions has been and continues to be expressed concerning the origins of merkavah mysticism and the tributaries that fed it. On these issues, see the suggestions for study on pages 62-63). Instructive throughout Kraemer's analysis are her caution about assumptions regarding dating and provenance, her respect for different recensions as windows into various communities, and her comments regarding the difficulties of establishing an original text. However, without a careful rebuttal of Burchard's textual arguments, her case is only suggestive, and seems too often to rest on personal opinion and assertion. The inductive approach is helpful as a supplement to text-critical analysis, but is (in my view) not a replacement for it. Burchard's careful arguments for the superiority of the *b* text therefore remain unparalleled by a counter-response for the *d* recension.

Burchard: Text-Critical Arguments for an Eclectic Text

Here are several of the reasons given by Burchard and others that have compelled scholars to accept the longer text. First, Burchard questioned Philonenko's overall view of textual development. Philonenko had traced the textual history as beginning with the short *d*, moving on to an expanded *b*, then to a revised *c*, and finally to the lengthy, polished *a*. There were several problems with this reconstruction. A careful examination of the differences in length and wording in the different text-types showed that *a*, for example, was more similar to *d* than to *b* or *c* in many respects, which should not be the case if the two families represented the first and last stages in development. Again, Philonenko himself had been constrained, in the preparation of his edition, to include some passages from the longer text to supplement his use of *d*, because it was clear from the state of *d* that there had been some abbreviation. If the text showed signs of abbreviation here and there, then why not elsewhere, or generally (i.e. it is an epitome)? Moreover, it seemed that Philonenko had confused two characteristics of family *a*—its length and its style—and had been influenced by his view of *a* when deciding about *b*. The reasoning ran as follows: *a* was manifestly a secondary version, since it had smoothed the archaising language of *Aseneth*; *a* and *b* were both lengthy; therefore neither could be considered as representative of an early text. It is clear, however, that similar length does not imply a similar character. Finally, Burchard mounted a strong series of arguments showing why it is more likely that *d* has omitted phrases or sections, rather than that *a* and *b* have added to or expanded the text. This included not simply the application of various critical tests to the readings (e.g. the principle that the *lectio difficilior* should be followed: a more 'difficult' or 'problematic' reading is likely to be prior, since redactors will smooth out difficulties rather than create them) but also consideration of the general rule that epitomes tend to abridge the last chapters or the final verses of a subsection, as *d* in fact does. As for family *b*, it includes the oldest witnesses to the text, and is a very large group, spread over different areas.

Unfortunately, Burchard has to this date not yet been able to produce the promised critical edition of his reconstructed text, which is based mostly on the *b* family. The Greek text that he published provisionally in the European journal *Dielheimer Blätter zum Alten Testament* is not easily accessible, and was produced with neither variants nor even aspiration and accents; these latter have been supplied in the copy reproduced in Denis's *Concordance*, but since there is as yet no apparatus, the text remains preliminary. Those who are interested in important variants may, however, consult the helpful notes added to his English *OTP* translation. Philonenko's version based on *d*, then, remains the only annotated text easily accessible to those who wish to study *Aseneth*, while the most common English translation and introduction is that of Burchard, based on a modified *b*. An English translation of the shorter text has been made by D. Cook, and is available in Sparks, *The Apocryphal Old Testament* (See 'Further Reading' pp. 27-28, for full references to these works.)

The delay in the publication of a complete edition may be due to Burchard's awareness that the establishment of the text remains a difficult and somewhat speculative venture: there is just so much we do not know about the development of the traditions and the interrelationships of the text-types. Indeed, Burchard has most recently confessed to some concern regarding the integrity of the *b* family, upon which his eclectic text is based. He wonders, in a 1987 article ('The Present State of

Research on Joseph and Aseneth', in J. Neusner *et al.* [eds.], *New Perspectives on Judaism*. II. *Religion, Literature and Society in Ancient Israel, Formative Christianity and Judaism* [2 vols.; Lanham, MD: University Press of America], pp. 31-52) whether further research into *b* might demonstrate new families, or subgroups. Nor is he under any illusions concerning the temporal distance between the families we possess and the original composition, which he has been trying to approximate. For some scholars who are sceptical about the possibility of such reconstruction, or who even argue that no single *Ur*-text and author ever existed, Burchard's reserve is telling. On the other hand, the artistry and integrity of the story (particularly in its *b* form) is remarkable, and militates against the dubious scenario of a work composed by committee in ancient times. *Aseneth* is no folk-work, with its sophisticated use of biblical and Hellenistic traditions, and its incorporation of these into a compelling and coherent whole. Although the last word has not been given in the debate over text-types, Burchard's departure point from the *b* text is sane, and has not inconsiderable support.

The Narrative Integrity of the Longer Text

Most important for the present author is the crucial character quality of the central revelatory section (chs. 14–17), which in its abbreviated *d* form lacks dramatic weight, sequential integrity and the power to inform other passages in *Aseneth*. Missing from *d* (but present in the *b* family) are several pregnant key passages. First, the short text omits the passage concerning the heavenly Visitor's name (15.11-12 in Burchard's text), a sequence that provides the structural core of the visionary section. Again, the short text makes no link between the female heavenly figure Metanoia with this unnamed Visitor (15.8). This is important since the heavenly liaison provides a mystical complement to the spousal-sibling connection of Joseph and Aseneth (cf. 7.8; 21.4). Also missing are the mysterious description of the bees and various details about the honeycomb (16.17y-23 in Burchard), which seem extraneous and inexplicable if viewed as additions in a longer text, but which an editor, impatient with the lengthy epiphany, might easily have dropped. Again, the building of a honeycomb on Aseneth's lips, which enhances the heroine's status as City of Refuge, finds no place in the short text, nor does the division of the bees into friendly and hostile attendants of Aseneth—a detail that prefigures the action sequel to the story in several ways. Finally, adjacent to the vision proper, and providing a natural climax towards which the vision builds, is the full-blown description of Aseneth's transformation, found only in the longer text. This dramatic conclusion to the epiphany, a confirmation of her change in status, is severely abbreviated, almost glossed, in the short text. Other observations about the whole narrative are pertinent. In the short text, several balancing passages are missing, including triple sequences that permeate the story in the longer text. In the latter, these triple formulae are set off by Joseph's prayer (8.9) for Aseneth, which has a threefold form (invocation of the living God, requested blessing of life for Aseneth and supplication for Aseneth's future eternal life), and provides a threefold promise ('let her eat of your bread of life, and drink your cup of blessing, and number her among your people'). As we follow Aseneth through her adventure, these themes and promises are sustained and confirmed at crucial points in the longer text. First, Joseph confers the blessing and promise (8.9), then the Visitor reaffirms that Aseneth will in fact enjoy this fate: 'Behold, from today you will be renewed and formed anew and made alive again, and you will eat blessed bread of life, and drink a blessed cup of immortality and anoint yourself with blessed ointment of incorruptibility' (15.5.) Aseneth, on being fed with the honeycomb, is told that she has enjoyed the eternal benefits of the food, drink and unction of the elect (16.16); at her reunion with Joseph, she is given a threefold embrace that communicates life, wisdom and truth (19.11); and in the final sequences, during the family meal and the wedding, emphasis is placed several times on Aseneth's transformative beauty, and the power of God to give life to the dead (20.5; 20.7; 21.4). Most of these elements are missing (excised?) from the short version. The consistency of these themes and their dramatic deployment at various moments in the story are underscored by the structure and motifs of Aseneth's Psalm (21.10-21), which closes the first narrative. As might be expected, this poetic coda is also missing from the shorter texts.

Consonant with these solemnly structured passages are other details found in the longer version, but absent in the short text. The short text features only one penitential prayer of Aseneth and misses the two false starts of the longer text (11.3; 11.16; 12.1—again, a series of three!) In the short text, her maidens are blessed rather peremptorily as an appendix to the visionary section (17.5 in Philonenko); in the longer version, they are given places as 'pillars' in the City of Refuge (17.5-6 in Burchard), and seem to prefigure others who will find shelter there. Missing from the short text is the reason Aseneth gives for her Visitor to accept hospitality—*'so that I will know that you will do all that you have spoken to me'* (15.13). This theme is picked up again by the revelator at the end of the signs sequence (17.1-4) in the long version, but appears abruptly and rather fortuitously in its parallel place in the short text. The shorter version similarly finishes by describing the signs as confirmatory, but does not carefully introduce them in this manner as does the longer text at 15.13. Moreover, in the longer version, where Joseph and Aseneth are reunited, the short text joins them without ceremony, simply with the comment that Joseph has 'had good news about [Aseneth] from heaven, explaining everything about [her]' (19.3, Philonenko's text). By contrast, the longer version has Joseph reiterate a major question from the revelatory section ('Who are you?') that Aseneth herself answers with flair (19.4-7). Her self-identification amounts to a rehearsal of the visionary experience, through which she has found a new identity, and highlights her new status as bride and City. During this speech, Aseneth also calls attention to Joseph's off-stage parallel epiphany, highlighting the well-known novelistic feature of double-visions, and the discourse closes with Joseph confirming her new appearance and new identity (19.8-9).

Such balancing characteristics *may* be the fruit of hard work by a later redactor, who was responsible for the *b* archetype (as reconstructed by Burchard), and who greatly enhanced the quality of a piece that came to hand. However, the details seem to flow naturally and creatively from the story itself. Their explanation in terms of elaboration is thus less likely than their omission by a redactor who found mystery irritating, wanted to get on with the story and was not aware of the subtle connections of the central section with the whole text. Gideon Bohak, another scholar who concentrates on this enigmatic episode, demonstrates significant textual incoherence and awkwardness in the shorter text's honeycomb sequence, and notes how its prefiguring technique is neutralized by the absence of key phrases (*Joseph and Aseneth and the Jewish Temple in Heliopolis* [Early Judaism and its Literature, 10; Atlanta: Scholars Press, 1996], pp 106-109). Some of his arguments are more compelling if one accepts his unusual view of the book (discussed later) but many of its details remain significant even if one has a different or broader understanding of how *Aseneth* functions.

All this is not to say that there is no reason to analyse the story as it appears in its shorter version(s). It would perhaps be an exaggeration to consider the shorter text a work in its own right, since it lacks the integrity of the longer version. On the other hand, the shorter recension favoured by Philonenko clearly is no mere abbreviation, but represents the telling of *Aseneth* in a different mode. Here the slowing of the pace during the penitential and revelatory section is far less noticeable, and many of the esoteric details are not stressed. As a result, the popular and novelistic quality of *Aseneth* emerges, while the revelatory characteristic of the piece is rather muted. While the longer version includes many revelatory (im)ponderables, in the shorter version neither the mystery of the Visitor, nor the new luminosity of Aseneth are stressed. The lack of repetitive phrases to signal structure, such as are present in the longer text, makes an argument about intentional (or inherent but unmistakable) artistry in the short text rather difficult to mount. However, the revelatory section, as it stands in the short version, does seem to give a greater prominence to the heavenly Metanoia. In noting this, along with other details, some have suggested that there is a consistent and discernible attitude towards the feminine in the shorter text. (See section 5 of this chapter).

Modus Operandi
Clearly, decisions about text are indissolubly bound up with more general issues of interpretation. It would be a simple affair if we had independent evidence for the best text and could move from there to various analyses of content: as the matter stands, the procedure is much more circular and reconstructive in nature. For the reasons that I have given above, I consider the longest text-type, approximated by Burchard's provisional eclectic text, to be normative, and will, unless I signal otherwise, be working from it; I will likewise, for the most part, make use of his English translation in *OTP*, except at a few points where I will offer my own rendering. Like Burchard, I consider that there was an original text, but that we have not retrieved it fully, and that there is much room for further analysis and discussion. Textual analysis of this sort is not necessarily (as Kraemer implies) fuelled by a quest for the 'true' or 'divinely inspired' text. (This would be an odd quest, considering that *Aseneth* has never enjoyed canonical status!) Indeed, those who are intrigued by the intrinsic artistry of a work may also insist that authorial intent is not irrelevant: from this perspective, decisions about an integrated text remain important.

To take Burchard's text as normative does not mean, however, that the shorter text-family is insignificant. Until recently those convinced by Burchard's arguments characteristically have made no attempt to treat the short text in any way (cf. my own *The Ladies and the Cities: Transformation and Apocalyptic Identity in Joseph and Aseneth, 4 Ezra, The Apocalypse and The Shepherd of Hermas* [JSPSup, 17; Sheffield: Sheffield Academic Press, 1995]). At the very least the recent work of Ross Kraemer and others indicates that this version is worth consideration, because of its unique tendencies and purposes—even if some continue to note its *manquée* quality. We may wonder, however, whether the current penchant for a multiplicity of texts is too often driven by an ideological or emotive reaction against 'hegemonic' claims for original or best texts. In the new orthodoxy, every voice must be allowed to speak. This claim is valuable when the purpose of the analysis is to trace different communities that have read and transmitted a text. In this case, there would be much to learn from a comparison of *b* with *d* (and indeed with every recension available!) Various modes of text may be for the historian windows into the concerns and assumptions of different communities that knew *Aseneth*, although this is a quest fraught with difficulties. However, where the particular quest is to hear, understand and appreciate an integrated text (which has incidentally been transmitted in briefer recensions), then the subsequent history is less important, except for purposes of contrast. Most of the analysis here will therefore concern the longer text as reconstructed by Burchard, and translated in the *OTP*. Where it is necessary or helpful to note variances in the shorter text (e.g. in the discussion of feminist readings), I will refer to *Aseneth (P)*, making use of Philonenko's Greek text and citing the English translation by D. Cook, which is easily accessible in Sparks, *Apocryphal Old Testament*.

Further Reading

Arguments for *d* Family

Kraemer, Ross Shepard, *When Aseneth Met Joseph: A Late Antique Tale of the Biblical Patriarch and his Egyptian Wife, Reconsidered* (New York: Oxford University Press, 1998). Kraemer presents her arguments in the introduction, pp. 6-9, and through a comparative reading of the texts in Chapters 2 and 3 of her work.

Philonenko, Marc, *Joseph et Aséneth: Introduction, texte critique, traduction et notes* (SPB, 13; Leiden: E.J. Brill, 1968).

Arguments for *b* Family

Burchard, C, *Untersuchungen zu Joseph und Aseneth* (WUNT, 8; Tübingen: J.C.B. Mohr [Paul Siebeck], 1965). Burchard's careful investigation of the apocryphon includes a full discussion of the textual traditions on pp. 18-90.

—'Zum Text von "Joseph und Aseneth" ', *JSJ* 1 (1970), pp. 3-34. Burchard rebuts Philonenko's arguments for the short text and presents arguments for an eclectic text.

Bohak, Gideon, *Joseph and Aseneth and the Jewish Temple in Heliopolis* (Early Judaism and its Literature, 10; Atlanta: Scholars Press, 1996). Bohak presents a novel reading of the apocryphon, but in an appendix, pp. 106-109, explains why his reading supports Burchard's view of a longer text-type.

Chesnutt, Randall D., *From Death to Life: Conversion in Joseph and Aseneth* (JSPSup, 16; Sheffield: Sheffield Academic Press, 1995). Chesnutt's informative reading includes a full examination of the textual issues, and cogently champions Burchard's text. See especially pp. 36-43 and 65-69.

Humphrey, E.M., *The Ladies and the Cities: Transformation and Apocalyptic Identity in Joseph and Aseneth, 4. Ezra, The Apocalypse and the Shepherd of Hermas* (JSPSup, 17; Sheffield: Sheffield Academic Press, 1995). Demonstrates the structural coherence of the longer text.

Discussions of the Difference between the Two Texts

Burchard, C., 'The Present State of Research on Joseph and Aseneth', in J. Neusner *et al.* (eds.), *New Perspectives on Judaism. II. Religion, Literature and Society in Ancient Israel, Formative Christianity and Judaism* (2 vols.; Lanham, MD: University Press of America, 1987), pp. 31-52.

Kraemer, Ross Shepard, *When Aseneth*, Chapters 2–3.

Standhartinger, Angela, *Das Frauenbild im Judentum der hellenistischen Zeit: Ein Beitrag anhand von 'Joseph und Aseneth'* (Arbeiten zur Geschichte des antiken Judentums und des Urchristentums, 26; Leiden: E.J. Brill, 1995). Standhartinger argues on pp. 219-25 for the integrity of both texts, and insists that the shorter text is no abridgement. Her conclusions are applied (in tentative English) to a close comparison of several sections in 'From Fictional Text to Socio-Historical Context', in *SBLSP 1996* (Atlanta: Scholars Press, 1996), pp. 302-18.

Greek Texts

Batiffol, P., *Le livre de la prière d'Aséneth* (Studia Patristica: Études d'ancienne littérature chrétienne, 1–2; Paris: Leroux, 1889–90). Greek based on family *a*, plus Latin version.

Burchard, C., 'Ein vorläufiger griechischer Text von *Joseph und Aseneth*', *DBAT* 14 (1979), pp. 2-53; and 'Verbesserungen zum vorläufigen Text von Joseph und Aseneth', *DBAT* 16 (1982), pp. 37-39. Burchard's reconstructed eclectic text, leaning on family *b*.

Denis, A.-M., OP, *Concordance grecque des pseudépigraphes d'Ancien Testament: Concordance, corpus des textes, indices*, avec la collaboration d'Yvonne Janssens et le concours du CETEDOC (Louvain-la-Neuve: Université Catholique de Louvain, 1987). Denis reproduces Burchard's provisional text, adding aspiration and accents.

Philonenko, Marc, *Joseph et Aséneth: Introduction, texte critique, traduction et notes* (SPB, 13, Leiden: E.J. Brill, 1968). Philonenko's Greek text is based on family *d*.

English Translations of Aseneth

Burchard, C., 'Joseph and Aseneth', pp. 177-247. An English translation of the eclectic text, with two versification systems.

Cook, D. 'Joseph and Aseneth', in H.F.D. Sparks (ed.), *The Apocryphal Old Testament* (Oxford: Clarendon Press, 1984), pp. 465-503. Cook's English translation follows Philonenko's text.

2. Provenance and Date

Early Views

Connected with the issue of text have been the questions of provenance and date. *Aseneth* was for some time given a date several centuries into the common era, and assumed to be a Christian production, through deference to the Byzantinist P. Batiffol (*La prière d'Aséneth*, pp. 7-18, 30-37). For him the Christian quality of the work was discernible in its allusive symbolism (pp. 19-29). Particularly, he saw in the figure of Joseph a representation of Christ, and in Aseneth a complex figure of 'la virginité', the Church and the fervent (and traditionally feminine) figure who prays (*Orans*). The extended penitential section, Aseneth's conversion and the poignant 'sacramental' passages suggested to him that this work was concerned with Christian initiation. Details such as the Visitor's instruction for Aseneth to remove her veil further confirmed this impression, since Batiffol connected this with Montanist controversies, citing Tertullian's *On the Veiling of Virgins*. (He also saw this as reason to place the writing in Asia Minor, whence the movement originated.) In his decision about the Christian character of *Aseneth*, Batiffol did not depart radically from those who had examined the document (but less thoroughly) in the century before his time.

What made his analysis unique was the perception that *Aseneth*, as we have it, was a Christian reworking of the Jewish 'haggadic' story (of which only traces remain) of Aseneth, the daughter of Dinah. (*Haggada* may be loosely defined as instruction through—sometimes fanciful—narrative, as opposed to *halaka*, instruction through precept or command.) This Hebrew tale provided the basis for rabbinic stories still extant in later sources, and sought to explain how the faithful Joseph could have married one who *seemed* to be a Gentile. Aseneth was none other than the illegitimate, but therefore partly Hebrew, child of Dinah, who had been violated by Shechem. (We might also comment that Genesis 34 concerns the questions of interrelationships between circumcised and uncircumcised, and so provides, between its lines, a natural *entrée* for such a tale.) Batiffol reasoned that since the haggada could be dated to the fourth century CE, the reworked Christian story must be about a century later: thus he arrived at a fifth-century date.

The scholarly community was not, however, to retain Batiffol's identification of *Aseneth* as late, Christian and from Asia Minor. He was immediately criticized from various quarters, and Batiffol himself soon conceded that the original writing of *Aseneth* could have been earlier, and even by a Jewish writer (*RB* 7 [1898], pp. 302-304). V. Apotowitzer went on to build upon Batiffol's detection of the haggadic background and suggested that *Asenath* (*sic*, cf. the Hebrew Bible vocalization) had originally been written in Hebrew, in the first century CE, and had then been translated into Greek by a Hellenistic Jew who saw its proselytizing potential. As the piece became popular among Christians, who reinterpreted and expanded its symbolism, it dropped out of favour in Jewish circles.

Aptowitzer's views, especially his contention that the piece was originally written in Hebrew, were no more compelling to most scholars than the early ones of Batiffol. Nevertheless, the character of the piece, as Jewish or Christian, continued to be debated; noteworthy is Ross Kraemer's observation that Jewish scholars have preferred a Jewish authorship, while Christians have tended more towards a Christian milieu (*When Aseneth*, p. 231). The first half of this statement is demonstrable; there are, however, a majority of non-Jewish scholars who maintain that the author of *Aseneth* was a Hellenistic Jew writing for a Hellenistic Jewish audience. As to dating, scholars now generally place the piece in an era much earlier than the fifth century, many looking towards the late first century CE as the most likely time of composition. The first-century CE date is usually given as a *terminus ante quem* because the apocryphon is judged to be of Egyptian origin: a Jewish community in Egypt would have little use for a pro-proselyte book like *Aseneth* after the revolt under Trajan in 117, or especially after Hadrian's anti-circumcision edict in 135. Although the provenance of the work is problematic, given the original Egyptian setting of the Joseph story, various internal details make an Egyptian milieu plausible, if not probative. Many have cited the forceful repudiation of Egyptian gods described in well-known cultural terms, intimations of the Egyptian goddess Neith (in Aseneth's name and various details associated with her) and the solar deity Re (cf. the solar imagery at 5.4-5; 14.9; 17.8-9), the prominence of bee imagery, and various *realia* of furniture, clothing, agriculture, seasons, buildings, eating habits, and geography. More detailed links with particular social groupings (see in particular D. Sänger, *Antikes Judentum und die Mysterien: Religionsgeschichtliche Untersuchungen zu Joseph und Aseneth* [WUNT, 25; Tübingen: J.C.B. Mohr [Paul Siebeck], 1980] and Bohak, *Joseph and Aseneth*) and events in Egyptian history have also been cited, but have not been compelling to most scholars. While it is impossible to argue an absolute case for provenance on the basis of internal evidence alone, the Egyptian milieu seems most likely. If Egypt is accepted as a probable matrix, then the relation between Jews and Gentiles is helpful in determining date—some specialists have considered that a dating before the time in Egypt when hostilities escalated against the Jewish population (i.e. persecution in Alexandria in 38 CE) is preferable. Others have opted for an earlier date, on the basis that Rome is never mentioned, and because the Egypt of Aseneth is seemingly independent (i.e. in the Ptolemaic era before the Roman conquest of Egypt in 30 BCE). It is just as likely the case that the novel reflects the idyllic period of its biblical story when Hebrew and Gentile, and that it also yields no clear clues as to pre-Roman origin.

Affinities with the Septuagint

The original Greek character of the language is at least one point now virtually beyond dispute. Aptowitzer grounded his argument to the contrary on an analysis of the name of Aseneth and her new title 'City of Refuge'. He, along with L. Ginzberg (*The Legends of the Jews* [trans. H. Szold *et al.*; 7 vols.; Philadelphia: Jewish Publication Society, 1909–38], V, pp. 374-75) understood *Aseneth* 15.7 as a play on words: 'No longer shall your name be Aseneth, but your name shall be City of Refuge.' A link was seen between the Hebrew form of 'Asenath' (*'snat*) and various forms of the Hebrew roots 'to seek refuge' (*ḥsh*) and 'to be strong' (*ḥsn*), or the Aramaic noun (*ḥwsn'*) for 'fortress' or 'strength'. The proposals offered for understanding this verse are not consistent, and other variations, with the same purpose of establishing a Semitic prototype, have been suggested by other authors. More recently, for example, P. Riessler ('Joseph und Asenath. Eine altjüdische Erzählung', *TQ* 103 [1922], pp. 1-22, 145-83) suggested a connection of the name with the verb 'she fled' and cognates. This author has bolstered his view with an examination of difficult passages in the Greek manuscripts that he explains by reference to 'mistranslations' of an original Hebrew version. Riessler's citing of textual problems has not, however, convinced many of a Hebrew *Ur*-text. Moreover, his solution to the name-giving verse suffers by the presence of various other competing readings. The very multiplicity of solutions to 15.7, plus the strong possibility that a Greek-writing author may indeed have had enough Hebrew to reproduce a (now obscure) play on names, makes the argument for an original Hebrew rather weak.

On the other hand, there are compelling reasons to conclude that *Aseneth* was written originally in Greek. Most notable are the very many Septuagintal expressions and allusions, plus complex Greek words and phrases that point away from translation to an author well-versed in Greek, but using a biblicizing Greek informed by the LXX. Careful examination of the language and imagery of *Aseneth* shows direct dependence on the LXX (or a similar Old Greek version). For example, the comparison of LXX Psalm 18 with important themes and phrases in _Aseneth_ is instructive. Certain passages in _Aseneth_, such as the sun-chariot in _Aseneth_ 5.4 and 6.6 (cf. Ps. 19.4b-6) exhibit only a general or thematic likeness with the Psalm in its Hebrew form (Masoretic Text Psalm 19), but the verbal echoes that emerge from a comparison to the Greek rendering are striking. Other passages have been adduced to demonstrate dependence on other Septuagintal passages, such as _Aseneth_ 18.7-9 (cf. Song of Songs 4–5) and 15.6 (cf. Judges 13). In fact, evidence of _Aseneth_'s knowledge of the LXX, or another similar Greek version, has been suggested by so many independent studies, including the masterful article of G. Delling ('Einwirkungen der Sprache der Septuaginta in "Joseph und Aseneth" ', _JSJ_ 9 [1978], pp. 29-56), that it can hardly be ignored. Another supporting argument against an original Hebrew version is that the legendary treatment of Asenath in the haggada shows no knowledge whatever of our form(s) of the story, and provides an entirely different view of Joseph's wife. As an argument from silence this is not conclusive in itself, but adds to a cumulative case alongside strong Septuagintal echoes.

Specialists no longer, then, seriously debate the Septuagintal character of _Aseneth_. This factor gives us a rough lower bracket for the work, since it is highly unlikely that works influenced by the Greek version(s) could have been written prior to the mid second century BCE: some (e.g. Chesnutt, _From Death_, p. 80) would argue that Septuagintal echoes prevent a dating prior to the first century BCE. Our knowledge of the genesis of the LXX (and other Greek texts of the Old Testament), in its parts and in entirety, is not precise enough to be certain here, and scholars vary as to the appropriate amount of leniency at this point. It depends, of course, on whether one is arguing for a possible, or probable case of dating and provenance, how the LXX factor is to be considered. That is, one may confidently expect LXX echoes in the first century BCE; on the other hand, it is only possible that this influence could have been felt earlier; thus the burden of proof lies more heavily on a writer arguing for a prior date.

The Hellenistic character of _Aseneth_ and its dependence on an Old Greek version may, then, be regarded as established. However, the consensus concerning date and provenance has of late been challenged. This has taken place on two fronts, one scholar now arguing for a very early dating, while retaining the Egyptian milieu and Jewish Hellenistic character, and a few others leaning towards a much later date, questioning the Egyptian hypothesis, and moving back to the possibility of a Christian rather than Jewish author. We will see how these moves are interconnected with views about the long and short recensions, and about the importance (or otherwise) of establishing the earliest text.

Bohak: Aseneth as an Apocalyptic Justification of the Heliopolitan Temple

We begin with a consideration of Gideon Bohak's challenge to the consensus in *Joseph and Aseneth*. In concert with many of his peers, Bohak champions the longer text, not only because of the painstaking arguments of Burchard, but also (as we have seen) because of his analysis and view of the central revelatory section. He is alone in assigning so early a date for *Aseneth*, and we have yet to see how his views will be received by the scholarly community. In characteristic circular (though not necessarily vicious) fashion, Bohak's understanding of the apocryphon both depends upon and confirms an Egyptian provenance. He argues that *Aseneth* was written as an in-house *apologia* and justification for the alternate temple and cult that was established in Heliopolis by Onias IV and his supportive priests after Onias III had been murdered in Antioch around 171 BCE. These events are alluded to in such biblical and para-biblical texts as 1 Macc. 4.34, *1 En.* 90.8, Dan. 9.26 and 11.22 and described (with inner discrepancy) by Josephus in *War* 1.31-3 and *Ant.* 12.237 and 13.73, and later by Jerome in *Comm. in Dan.* 3.11.14. Despite the conflicting accounts and obscurity of Onias IV's flight, Bohak argues convincingly that we can understand the general historical situation that informs the writing of *Aseneth*. The young son of a high priest who has been cheated of his position in Jerusalem chooses Heliopolis as a place of refuge because of his community's prophetic reading of Isa. 19.18-19:

> On that day there will be five cities in the land of Egypt that…swear allegiance to the Lord of Hosts. One of these will be called the City of the Sun. On that day there shall be an altar to the Lord in the center of the land of Egypt

Ptolemy VI (Philometor) accepts the refugee and his followers, and enacts an alliance with them (protection and rights for military service and loyalty). This is (perhaps hyperbolically) described by Josephus in *Apion* 2.49. The renaming of Heliopolis as *Oniou* ('of Onias') bears a felicitous similarity to the ancient name of *On*, and so confirms the refugees in their ancient claim to the city.

The temple built in Heliopolis has not been recovered, despite arguments that it stood at Tell-el-Yahoudieh (Leontopolis). Nevertheless, there is ample written evidence of its existence, and it seems to have been patterned after the Jerusalem temple. Intriguingly, LXX readings of the key verse Isa. 19.18 have changed the title 'City of the Sun' to 'City of Righteousness'. Would Onias and his followers have read this to mean a transfer of the Isaianic promises to Jerusalem (Isa. 1.26) to the Egyptian site? It is along such lines, Bohak reasons, that *Aseneth* is to be understood. The book, though novelesque in its outer appearance, shelters a mystery and revelation in its central section. In particular, the enigmatic honeycomb passage in its longer version (*Aseneth* 16.8–16x) becomes the springboard for his thesis. This is a particularly attractive point of departure, since the passage remains unexplained by scholars of the apocryphon. In Bohak's reading, the bees' exotic attire (the colour and the materials) suggests a representation of Jewish priests, while a new honeycomb built on Aseneth's lips, and the combustion of the first comb, picture an alternate and transferred temple and cult. The burning of the comb may be construed as an example of *vaticinia ex eventu* (prophecy after the event) or as an actual anticipation (on the part of the Oniads who deplored corrupt Jerusalem) of the events in 70 CE. The two groups of bees, those friendly to Aseneth and those not, represent, alternatively, the supporters and detractors of the Heliopolitan temple, as do the friendly and hostile brothers of the second tale.

Bohak supports his exegesis by reference to passages and details outside of the revelatory section. For example, he links the constant references to Pentephres' 'field of inheritance' with the Heliopolitan home afforded Onias by Philometor ('returned' to the chosen people, since it had belonged to Aseneth and Joseph in the first place). Again, he explains the details of Pentephres's house by reference to details of the temple in Ezekiel 47 (spring, trees, fruit), its temple-like tower, complete with curtains, and the notion of 'graded holiness' whereby the inner sanctuary of Aseneth's room is depicted as the holy of holies. To this concept of temple holiness is added a consideration of Oniad eschatology, which would have centred its hopes on the Heliopolitan temple as the source of life for the remnant of pure Judaism and those repentant Gentiles who come to its light. All these details are worked together to suggest a surprising new *raison d'être* and dating for *Aseneth*. Here Bohak suggests two possibilities. First, the honeycomb episode *may* have been penned in the years between 70 and 74 CE (i.e. after the destruction of the Jerusalem temple, but before the unanticipated fall of the Oniad temple) by those who saw in the Heliopolitan cult the hope of the future. More likely, however, the book was composed at a much earlier time, in the mid-second century BCE, as an explanatory and polemical 'revelation' of the newly established cult in Heliopolis.

Kraemer: Aseneth as a Product of Late Antiquity

For Bohak the episode of the bees is the key to the purpose of the book, to its peculiar Jewish authorship, and to its early original dating; for Ross Kraemer, 'the drama of the bees is…the drama of the fate of souls' which finds its 'closest identifiable analogue in third century Neo-Platonic sources' (*When Aseneth*, p. 295). We have seen already that Kraemer champions the shorter text-type as the earlier version, although she has an aversion to 'the frustrating pursuit of elusive 'original' texts' (p. 305). Even the 'earlier' short text-type is, however, most likely a late production. In her view, the common arguments for early dating are connected in circular fashion to an Egyptian provenance and an original Jewish (though Hellenistic) author. She seeks, then, to 'dismantle' these links, arguing that *Aseneth* may just as easily be the product of a Christian (or other) milieu, that the Egyptian provenance is not the only or best option and that even a Jewish origin is better explained in terms of a third century or later *Sitz im Leben*. Kraemer, while aware of the natural 'resistance' of pseudepigraphic texts to dating and classification, nevertheless is 'personally comfortable with the conclusion that *Aseneth* is much more likely to have been composed no earlier than the third century C.E.' (p. 304). Further, though she says it is impossible to be certain, the rhetorical direction of her parallels leads away from Jewish authorship and in the direction of a Christian, 'theosebic' (or even Samaritan) origin, with (perhaps) a provenance in Syria or Asia Minor. The major purpose of Kraemer's recent volume is not only, then, to cast doubt upon the scholarly consensus, but to rehabilitate the older view of *Aseneth* as a product of late antiquity, as made clear in her subtitle. Batiffol's instincts were right, though his arguments were faulty.

Assessing the Dispute

These newest analyses have challenged the two-hundred-year consensus regarding dating, with Bohak's hypothesis pulling the time of origin back to the mid-second century BCE and Kraemer's reading stretching it forward to the third century CE or even later. The major obstacle to Bohak's thesis has already been intimated, that is, the availability of the LXX to inform the text at his favoured date. His second option of 70–74 CE would allow for confidence regarding Septuagintal influence, but does not fit the Ptolemaic context for which Bohak argues painstakingly from the details surrounding the friendly pharaoh and Joseph's militaristic brothers. At any rate, an adequate assessment of

Bohak's work depends upon a consideration not only of plausible dates, but of his thesis as a whole, including his view of the genre of *Aseneth*, especially its central revelatory section, his acceptance of the longer recension, and his use of various details in the book to establish the Oniads' purpose. Those weighing the evidence will have to decide whether Bohak's solution to the riddle of the bees is adequately supported by the overall reading, and then deal with our limited knowledge of the emerging Septuagint.

Kraemer's proposed late dating initially may seem less audacious than Bohak's thesis, since she professes a wise agnosticism at several points, is unconcerned about the original text, and is prepared to entertain several plausible communities as the matrices or nourishers of the story. However, to treat *Aseneth* as a late (plausibly Christian) antique tale, alongside disparate Neo-Platonic and late merkavah parallels, is in itself a bold move, as is the championing of Philonenko's recension without the support of a systematic textual analysis. Kraemer herself recognizes that scholars are likely to 'continue to resist the rethinking' (p. 238) that her conclusions require; students of the apocryphon will have to examine the force of Kraemer's own arguments to decide whether such resistance would be arbitrary and stubborn, or whether her inductive approach is insufficient to challenge the prevailing views.

Of importance in this discussion is the recognition of our limitations but growing capacity to reconstruct the Judaism(s)—including earliest Christianity—of the early centuries of the common era. Many of Kraemer's arguments for a later date stem from the fact that we cannot confidently assign earlier dates to merkavah materials. Yet more and more evidence suggests that transformational mysticism was no late theme, but one known, promoted and reacted to in writings far earlier than the third and fourth centuries CE. Increasing work on the Qumran material, on the experiences and polemic of the apostle Paul, on the multiplicity of views regarding angels and eschatology, and on the wider range of Judaisms in the first century of our era suggest that transformation was a hope that made a very early appearance, though it was not accepted or stressed in all quarters. (Those interested in these matters can consult the suggested readings on pp. 62-63). A strength of both Kraemer and Bohak is that they have remained sensitive to the revelatory character of *Aseneth*, a characteristic that has sometimes been overlooked when scholars have assumed that the book is 'about' the acceptance of proselytes, and representative of 'non-sectarian' Judaism (whatever that may mean when dealing with a formative and fluid period).

It is essential in making any tentative decision regarding dating and provenance to acknowledge the uncertainties surrounding pseudepigraphic writings, and to consider various possibilities alongside a sensitive reading of the whole of *Aseneth*. The difficulty with Bohak's argument, as it stands, is that it tends to reduce the romance to a single purpose, an *apologia* for the alternate temple—the continued appreciation of *Aseneth* in various forms beyond its first audience (whatever that was) shows that the piece cannot be so reduced. The problem with Kraemer's analysis is that it adduces numerous parallels within what she envisages as a very fluid religious scene, with easy commerce between faiths—this, at the very time (according to her reckoning) when we know that Christian and rabbinic Jewish identities were being crystallised. Further, her reading of *Aseneth* seems to subordinate the inner mysteries of the text to theurgic manipulation, a practice that Kraemer believes was everywhere present in *late* antiquity. Yet it is not at all clear that Kraemer has effectively closed the door to an earlier dating, nor completely understood the force of the mysticism in this beguiling story.

Perhaps we will not agree with Bohak that it is necessary to nail down the date and provenance to appreciate this work, although some will find his reading of the honeycomb episode intriguing. Again, we may not be convinced by Kraemer that the work can find no home in pluriform first-century Judaism (or earlier). The very comfort of the Christian community with a piece that shows no irrefutable evidence of Christian normalization suggests that *Aseneth* comes from a period before the 'parting of ways', and before nascent rabbinic Judaism and Christianity established their own distinct practice, theology and liturgy. At any rate, the interconnection of issues—text-type, dating, provenance, original faith community—has become apparent as we have struggled with newer views. In this seamless robe of analysis, it is imperative to move beyond a discussion of dating and provenance to a consideration of genre: what kind of work is this much-disputed apocryphon?

Further Reading

On the Septuagint

Delling, G. 'Einwirkungen der Sprache der Septuaginta in "Joseph und Aseneth" ', *JSJ* 9 (1978), pp. 29-56. A careful examination of the LXX's influence upon Aseneth.

Müller, Mogens, *The First Bible of the Church: A Plea for the Septuagint* (JSOTSup, 206; Sheffield: Sheffield Academic Press, 1996). A helpful introduction to the history and influence of the LXX.

On the Jewish Haggada

Ginzberg, L., *The Legends of the Jews* (trans. H. Szold *et al.*, 7 vols.; Philadelphia: Jewish Publication Society, 1909-38).

Kraemer, Ross Shepard, *When Aseneth Met Joseph: A Late Antique Tale of the Biblical Patriarch and his Egyptian Wife, Reconsidered* (New York: Oxford University Press, 1998). See the appendix, pp. 307-21, which compiles various traditions about Aseneth and explains the complexities of dating and text. A useful anthology and commentary, regardless of one's views on the dating of *Aseneth*.

Neusner, Jacob, *Genesis Rabbah: The Judaic Commentary to the Book of Genesis: A New American Translation* (BJS, 106; 3 vols.; Atlanta: Scholars Press, 1985). *Aseneth* is mentioned in *Gen. R.* 85.2; 86.3; 97.

Contrasting Views of Provenance and Date

Batiffol, P., *Le livre de la prière d'Aséneth* (Studia Patristica: Études d'ancienne littérature chrétienne, 1-2; Paris: Leroux, 1889-90). Batiffol was responsible for the earliest view that *Aseneth* was a Byzantine Christian work.

Bohak, Gideon, *Joseph and Aseneth and the Jewish Temple in Heliopolis* (Early Judaism and its Literature, 10; Atlanta: Scholars Press, 1996). Bohak is unique in arguing for a mid-second century BCE date.

Chesnutt, Randall D., *From Death to Life: Conversion in Joseph and Aseneth* (JSPSup, 16; Sheffield: Sheffield Academic Press, 1995). Chesnutt presents a comprehensive discussion of the various views (omitting that of Kraemer, which appeared after his volume) and gives reasons for the prior 'consensus' of a date 100 BCE to 120 CE.

Kraemer, Ross Shepard, *When Aseneth*. Argues for a late (at least third-century CE) date for Aseneth, and disputes an Egyptian provenance.

Riessler, P., 'Joseph und Asenath. Eine altjüdische Erzählung', TQ 103 (1022), pp. 1-22, 145-83.

Sänger, D., *Antikes Judentum und die Mysterien: Religionsgeschichtliche Untersuchungen zu Joseph und Aseneth* (WUNT, 25; Tübingen: J.C.B. Mohr [Paul Siebeck], 1980).

3. Genre

The issue of genre is, in itself, and without reference to a complex book such as *Aseneth*, hotly debated today. In the wake of reader-oriented methods of reading has come a new self-consciousness about the process of inter-textual linking, its subjectivity and its polyvalent potential. Writings that may be fruitfully laid beside each other for analysis may be selected by reference to different sets of characteristics, so that a single work may be 'categorized' differently, depending upon the perspective. At any rate, the action of simply classifying works in a quasi-scientific manner has become suspect, since the sensitive reader will want to allow for the uniqueness of any text, as well as its similarities with others.

Again, theorists have been quick to point out that in previous discussions, generic categories have sometimes been described naively or carelessly so that they assume a 'reified' (rather than simply descriptive)

2. *Issues in Interpretation* 39

nature in the mind of the critic or reader. It is helpful, then, to cultivate a modest approach to generic distinctions that avoids the appearance of idealism—as if, for example, an 'apocalypse' were to be understood as something that exists 'out there' in pure form, against which all concrete examples are to be measured. Attention has also been paid to the maturation of a genre within a given society—haphazard though this may be— so that works may be discussed in terms of their naïveté (the conventions have not yet been fixed), their maturity (the conventions are well-known and used self-consciously by the author) and their sophistication (the conventions are so well-known that an author may test the limits of the genre). A full consideration of a work's genre would seek (where possible) to deal with the author and 'original context', the signals of the text and the efforts of initial and subsequent readers in recognizing and responding to these conventions or signals. That is, in a thorough analysis of genre, all three moments in the writing/text/reading process would come into play. Genre is thus considered as a heuristic category rather than as a merely classifying or restrictive factor. The sensitive critic seeks to name a work not to master, but to understand and befriend it. Indeed, as the Old Testament scholar John Barton insists, a provisional recognition of genre is an important first step in 'literary competence' (*Reading the Old Testament: Method in Biblical Study* [Louisville, KY: Westminster/John Knox Press, 1984 and 1996], Ch. 1); it is not, however, the last word in reading.

Aseneth and the Novel

When we turn to *Aseneth*, the complexities of classification and understanding become immediately apparent. In speaking to non-specialists about this piece, I have used the anachronism 'historical fiction' in order to evoke some of its flavour. To entertain by filling in the gaps of the Exodus story is, however, only one of the apparent impulses. *Aseneth* has notable affinities with biblical and deutero-canonical novellas (Esther, Ruth, Tobit, Judith), as well as with Hellenistic romances (e.g. the complete and fragmentary pieces of Chariton, Xenophon of Ephesus, Longus, Achilles Tatius and Heliodorus, as well as the tales of Lucius and Cupid and Psyche preserved by the Roman Apuleius in *Metamorphoses* 11 and 4–6 respectively). With many romantic novels, *Aseneth* shares an Egyptian milieu (perhaps a contraindication against actual Egyptian provenance?), a breathtakingly beautiful and tall heroine, and various complications of plot that are resolved. However, (most markedly in the longer text) our biblicizing novel combines with its intrigue and action a marked high-flown imagery and allusive mystery more often found in wisdom literature and in apocalypses. In this respect, *Aseneth* is even more difficult to characterize than other ancient novels, though the debate surrounding the origin and nature of that genre has been fierce enough. (See the illuminating survey of secondary literature by Richard I. Pervo, *Profit with Delight*, as detailed in 'Further Reading'.)

We find in *Aseneth*, then, various impulses at work: edification, diversion and mystical speculation. Such a confluence means that there continues to be much controversy among analysts beyond a general categorization of the piece as a romance or novel (terms that themselves are carefully distinguished by some specialists, but which are used as roughly equivalent by many, as they will be in this chapter). In an attempt at more precision within this general consensus, some have stressed the parallels to the *biblical* antecedents, calling attention to the prominence of the heroine, the 'exilic' setting and the relation between Jews and Gentiles. Others have been more taken with the *erotic* dimensions, and have highlighted the beauty and excellence of the heroine, her emotional response to the sight of Joseph, their separation, the obstacles to the match that are eventually overcome and (in the second story) the unsuccessful machinations of an evil suitor. This view has emerged in a reading of *Aseneth* as a Hellenistic romance with Jewish content. Alternatively, connection has been made to parallel motifs found in the Jewish '*sapiential* novels', such as Tobit, the court tales of Daniel 1–6 and *Ahiqar*. Again, it has been noted that the Hellenistic romance itself often served to propagate a religious *cult*: within this perspective, *Aseneth* fits well as a work commending a Judaism influenced by the mystery cults. Finally, the *Apocryphal Acts of the Apostles*, despite their lack of homogeneity, have been seen to have *thematic* connections, especially with the second part of *Aseneth*. Each of these approaches to the problem of genre has something to commend it, but fails to grasp all the characteristics of this intriguing book.

This difficulty in determining the most apt literary parallels is not limited to *Aseneth*. A reading of any piece—even of a fairly typical one—should take into account not only the characteristics that it shares with other works, but also its peculiarities. *Aseneth* is, however, 'more peculiar' than many writings. Obstinacy to generic classification is tied up with the difficulties already noted in these areas: recensions, *Sitz(e) im Leben*, function, and the faith community of writer, secondary writers or redactors, and primary as well as subsequent readers. We cannot be sure of authorial intention and influences beyond the biblical material, since we remain uncertain about the date. Moreover, the prospect is complicated because *Aseneth* is not a single narrative but a double tale, comprising chs. 1–21 and 22–29.

The Problem of Mysticism in the Two Tales of Aseneth

Initially, the first story seems more problematic. Critics have often stopped, nonplussed, at the appearance of an extended epiphany and revelation in chs. 14–17—a section that slows the action of the first story, and seemingly presents a symbolic and mystical detour. The reader of a romance is prepared to accept the parousia of an angelic figure as a device to remove the complications of the plot, and instate the heroine. But what is she or he to do with the multitude of seemingly gratuitous details that accompany his visitation—hidden manna-like honeycomb, description of beings in the heavens, formulaic oracles of acceptance, a sequence involving obscure bees whose significance Aseneth is supposed to grasp, but which eludes the casual reader? In the fifth section of this chapter, we will see that the disposition of these revelations is carefully arranged by chiasms in the longer version so as to call attention to the central mystery of the unnamed Visitor (15.11-12), a theme somewhat removed from Aseneth's own story. Moreover, the whole sequence compares aptly to the genre 'apocalypse' in mode, structure, content and function (see Humphrey, *The Ladies*, pp. 35-40 and Bohak, *Joseph and Aseneth*, pp. 17-18), while at the same time connecting easily with its host genre, the double novella of Aseneth's conversion and subsequent exploits. The unusual character of this revelatory sequence, and its careful integration within *Aseneth* have caused some to move beyond a broad categorization of novel or romance, in search of a literary form that more typically exhibits such features.

Those mysterious features that conspire to frustrate easy generic decisions are not confined to chs. 14-17, nor even to the first narrative, but cut across the subdivision at the end of ch. 21. Although the second narrative appears more adventure-oriented and less 'mystical' than the first, it is not devoid of such elements. Whereas in the first narrative there is a whole section devoted to the revelatory, in the second tale the mystic strain is more typically associated with characterization. For example, the priestly brother, Levi, is highlighted as Aseneth's special confidant, and a visionary who sees the secrets of human hearts and of the Most High:

> And Aseneth loved Levi exceedingly beyond all of Joseph's brethren, because he was one who attached himself to the Lord, and he was a prudent man and a prophet of the Most High and sharp-sighted with his eyes, and he used to see letters written in heaven by the finger of God and he knew the unspeakable (mysteries) of the Most High God and revealed them to Aseneth in secret, because he himself, Levi, would love Aseneth very much, and see her place of rest in the highest, and her walls like adamantine eternal walls and her foundations founded upon a rock of the seventh heaven (22.13).

These visionary characteristics of Levi are neither ornamental nor incidental, but essential in the shaping of the plot, as it unfolds and comes its conclusion. Aseneth's own character mirrors that of this prophet/priest whose hand she 'grasps' (22.12), as befits one who also is privy to the ineffable (16.12-14), and whose eternal place is in the heavens. At 27.10, it is her prayer, reminiscent of a high point in the first narrative (15.12), that catalyses a turning point in the action. That is, the Almighty responds immediately to Aseneth's own effective word, so that the conflict can move toward resolution:

> 'Lord my God, who made me alive again and rescued me...
> Rescue me from the hands of these wicked men.'
> And the Lord God heard Aseneth's voice, and at once their swords
> fell from their hands on the ground and were reduced to ashes (27.10-11).

The treacherous brothers interpret the event to mean that 'the Lord fights against us for Aseneth' (28.1), a phrase that associates the heroine with Joseph in the text itself (cf. 25.7) and also with biblical warriors who depend upon God. A host of biblical and deutero-canonical texts reproduce the phrase or the concept, as in Exod. 14.14, 25; Josh. 10.14, 23.10; Deut. 3.22; 2 Kgs 6.16; Neh. 4.14, 20; Jer. 21.5; Dan. 10.20; Jdt. 16.2; Sus. 59-60; 2 Macc. 3.25; and *3 Macc.* 6.18. While, in general dramatic terms, the Susanna episode seems most apposite (God responds to Susanna's cry, a response that is interpreted as his saving arm), Exod. 14.25 provides an exact parallel: here, the enemies of God's people recognize his protection of Israel: 'The Egyptians said: "The Lord is fighting for them against Egypt." ' It is interesting to note how the rôles have been reconstrued in our novel. Aseneth, the Egyptian who has joined herself to Israel, is saved from the hands of perfidious Israelites who have joined with Pharaoh's son; the Almighty fights for her against them.

The reader is not totally unprepared for this development. Aseneth has already been blessed with a new status in the first narrative, an identity that is confirmed by her significant visit to her 'father' Jacob at the beginning of the second story. If we follow Burchard's reconstructed text here (which depends on very early Syrian and Armenian texts, as well as a supporting later Latin manuscript, to fill in *lacunae* in the *b* family), the reversal of rôles and faithful agony of the heroine is prefigured. From the very outset of the second tale Aseneth is pictured as one 'sees' the eternal and who is—in some unspecified sense—like a warrior (22.7-9). A striking simile in the reconstructed v. 9 describes engaged attachment to the god-like Jacob; this is enriched by a prior reference (phrase reconstructed in v. 8) to Jacob as a mystic wrestler:

> And Aseneth saw [Jacob] and was amazed at his beauty… And Jacob was *like a man who had wrestled with God*… And Jacob called her to himself and blessed her and kissed her. And Aseneth stretched out her hands and grasped Jacob's neck and hung herself on her father's neck *just like someone hangs on to his father's neck when he returns from fighting* into his house, and she kissed him.

As the story unfolds, the reader comes to see that Aseneth's fighting strength rests in her faithful inner character. Like Levi, she exhibits forgiveness, repeating Levi's restraining words and exhibiting the power of her own right hand as she deals with brothers who are intent to avenge her honour (28.9, 14). She herself does not enter the fray, leaving this to the young Benjamin, but wields a power of word and presence. In this way, she assumes the same 'passive' strength as Esther and Susannah, although the emphasis upon her interior life is stronger. With Esther and Susannah, personal piety is emphasized, whereas with Aseneth, intimate knowledge of God's mysteries is stressed—a capacity acknowledged by the chief of hosts in the first narrative, and by the arch-priest/seer Levi in the second. The insight and generosity of Aseneth towards her assailants are intimately connected with the development and critical moments of the narrative. Aseneth now mirrors Joseph who in the first tale generously blessed Aseneth 'because of the great light…inside him' (6.6) and so initiated the action:

> And Joseph saw her, and had mercy on her exceedingly…because Joseph was meek and merciful and fearing God. And he lifted up his right hand and put it upon her head… (8.9).

At the commencement of *Aseneth*, Joseph the wise, by word and touch, extends blessing to the penitent Gentile Aseneth; at the conclusion, Aseneth displays her new nature as the mother of all those who seek refuge, taking under her wings by word and touch, not simply Gentiles (as we might have expected), but those who belong to Israel. Levi seals Aseneth's significant actions by kissing her right hand (28.16). We see, then, a dynamic of promise and fulfilment between the two

stories, as Aseneth's nature is declared in the first episode, but mani-
fested in the second. Of special interest is the manner in which the climax of the second story dramatizes the final enigmatic vision of the
first narrative's 'apocalypse'. At 16.18-23, two sets of bees, benevolent
and antagonistic, are nurtured by Aseneth. Aseneth, once incorporated
into Israel, has been so transformed as now to become herself an agent
of reconciliation within Israel. Such is the status of the one named
'City of Refuge' for '*all* who take refuge with the name of the Lord
God' (16.16).

The two tales, then, fit together as promise and fulfilment, although
the first has a conclusion proper to its own action. In terms of genre,
the first narrative displays many elements of an erotic romance.
However, it includes an emphasis on mysticism and conversion that
threatens to outweigh the love interest, inciting some to treat the material allegorically. Further, it plays host to extensive sapiential prayers of
confession (chs. 11–13), to a carefully structured hymnic epilogue (ch.
21) and to a chiastically framed apocalyptic sequence (chs. 14–17). The
second narrative seems at first to conform more readily to the 'adventure romance', but also exhibits anomalies. The scattered references to
contemplation, as seen in Jacob, Aseneth and Levi, at least distract the
reader from the action. All in all, Graham Anderson is accurate in his
declaration that *Aseneth* includes 'religious mystery for its own sake'
(*Ancient Fiction: The Novel in the Greco-Roman World* [London: Croom
Helm, 1984], p. 81); some readers, however, have been less negative
than Anderson in their appraisal of this characteristic within a novel.

Genre and Function
More is obviously going on here than a beguiling tale about the natu-
ralization of a beautiful and penitent Gentile, who becomes a fit wife
for Joseph and is subsequently rescued from dishonour. Nevertheless, it
is unwise to follow the conclusions of those who have seen in this
work a frank *roman à clef*, that is, a surface story to be decoded into a
specific message, be this initiation into a mystery religion or a specific
brand of Judaism (e.g. Essene, Therapeutic, Gnostic, merkavah mysticism). As we will see in the next section, such quests for specific cultic
clues have inevitably foundered. Indeed, the very presence of so many
'solutions' argues against an approach that tries to move from internal
details to specific external groups.

The evocative nature of *Aseneth* means, however, that some continue to search for a specific religious setting within which to place the

novel, and are thus influenced in their understanding of the book's genre. Others call attention to its artistry and insist that the book be read in aesthetic terms as a novel. In all this it is important to remember that the ancient world did not divide 'entertainment' from 'religious meaning' as we tend to today. Recent careful work by R.I. Pervo (see 'Further Reading', pp. 46-48) has suggested that the book is constructed syncretistically—in his view, as a reformulation of the biblical and deutero-canonical 'sapiential novel' to include romantic elements. However, authorial intent and the character of this piece as a naïve or sophisticated form of novel will remain somewhat elusive so long as we are uncertain both of the origin of the book and of the sources of mysticism in formative Judaism and early Christianity.

We must thus look at the cues within the book itself as primary evidence for its form and function, although such an investigation will remain somewhat circular: always we must interpret details within a particular work in relation to other pieces that we have already located, at least provisionally, in terms of date, provenance and genre. What remains evident is that the character traits and mystical propensities of the hero and heroine are drawn not simply to evoke awe and sympathy in the readers of this romance; similarly, the elusive passages, though unusual in a romance, do not stand out as foreign material. If the view taken here concerning recensions is correct, it would appear that the symbolic/wisdom/mystical material was of less importance than the story-line to at least one redactor. Perhaps this transmitter of the short text did not understand or appreciate these particular dimensions of the work; perhaps (s)he was reworking it for popular consumption, drastically reducing the symbolic elements, and enhancing its novelistic character. Yet even in this abbreviated form, the work led Philonenko to look beyond the categories of a popular biblicizing romance. Clearly, the esoteric details are inextricably integrated with the characterization and structure of the book—and this far more successfully in longer version.

In the end, *Aseneth* cannot be demonstrated to be 'about' initiation into a particular movement, nor about the happy possibility of pagans joining Israel. Nor is it simply 'about' the complication of a romance between Jew and Gentile, and how this is solved. Rather, the tale is spun, drawing us into it, all the while speaking in an allusive and entertaining way about the composition and nature of God's people. The identity of this people is connected in an intriguing manner with the unseen world, with ineffable and named figures such as Metanoia; surprisingly, God's community is also given an intensely practical dimension, as the key characters model what 'befits' one who 'fears God' and the appropriate relation between those within and without. Yet these 'messages' do not rob the plot of its power as a romance, nor subdue the story so that it becomes a mere prop for moral teaching. What emerges is unique configuration of material, manner, style and structure (for this 'formula', see Pervo, *Profit*, p. 114, and A.R. Heiserman, *The Novel before the Novel* [Chicago: University of Chicago Press, 1977], p. 59) that must be read, and not reduced to a single statement of purpose. *Aseneth*, then, is seen fruitfully as a 'romance with a difference'. At times that difference will be illuminated by reference to works that are neither romantic nor novelistic. It is wise, however, not to remain so long in such comparisons that the charm is scoured from *Aseneth*'s face, and she is banished from the world of story altogether. When we consider the unique configuration and integrity of this unusual piece, we need not be surprised that it has had such a long and broad life of transmission, for these features made it adaptable to various situations.

Further Reading

Genre

Barton, John, *Reading the Old Testament; Method in Biblical Study* (Louisville, KY: Westminster/John Knox Press, 1984 and 1996). Barton is convincing in his insistence that 'literary competence' begins with the recognition of genre. The entire book is sane in its approach to the reading of ancient literature, and is particularly helpful in its new edition, which has added chapters on reader–response and structuralism. See especially chapter 1, which is a good introduction to the question of genre.

Dubrow, H., *Genre* (London: Methuen, 1992). Dubrow coins the term 'host genre' in order to explain the phenomenon of ancient composite texts and their treatment by modern critics.

Fowler, A., 'The Life and Death of Literary Forms', *NLH* 2 (1971), pp. 199-216. This article offers a three-phase developmental theory that helps to explain composite texts.

Hellenistic Novels

Anderson, G., *Ancient Fiction: The Novel in the Greco-Roman World* (London: Croom Helm, 1984). A comprehensive work, dealing with character, structure, content and mode of the Hellenistic novels, but with a tendency to dismiss popular novels such as *Aseneth* as 'crude'. Anderson's devalues, for example, the Visitor's mediating interpretation of visionary details (p. 82), probably because he neglects the apocalyptic aspects of *Aseneth*, thus seeing the apocryphon as a decadent romance.

Grottanelli, C., 'The Ancient Novel and Biblical Narrative', *Quaderni urbinati di cultura classica* NS 27 (1987), pp. 7-34. A historian of religion makes helpful connections between the ancient novel and the biblical narratives.

Hägg, Tomas, *The Novel in Antiquity* (Berkeley: University of California Press, ET 1983 [1980]). This readable survey is extremely valuable and stresses the importance of the early popular novels.

Heiserman, Arthur Ray, *The Novel before the Novel* (Chicago: University of Chicago Press, 1977).

Pervo, R.I., 'The Ancient Novel: Its Origins and Nature' and 'Historical Novels: Pagan, Jewish and Christian', in *idem, Profit with Delight: The Literary Genre of the Acts of the Apostles* (Philadelphia: Fortress Press, 1987), pp. 86-135. Pervo's discussion is incomparable, giving a sane critique of such influential scholars as Rohde, Kerenyi, Merkelbach, Reardon, Anderson and Perry.

Reardon, B.P. (ed.), *Collected Ancient Greek Novels* (Berkeley: University of California Press, 1989). Reardon has gathered five 'greats' (Chariton, Xenophon of Ephesus, Longus, Achilles, Tatius and Heliodorus) and fragments, dated from the first to third centuries CE.

Apocalypses and Visionary Literature

Bloomquist, L. Gregory, and Greg Carey (eds.), *Vision and Persuasion: Rhetorical Dimensions of Apocalyptic Discourse* (St. Louis, MO: Chalice Press, 1999). Groundbreaking articles that examine the rhetorical tendencies of apocalyptic and revelatory writings from different perspectives.

Charlesworth, J.H., and J.J. Collins (eds.), *Mysteries and Revelations: Apocalyptic Studies since the Uppsala Colloquium* (JSPSup, 9; Sheffield: JSOT Press, 1991). Studies on genre, social movements and function in the apocalypses, many of which build on the two Semeia volumes listed below.

Collins, John J., 'Introduction: Towards the Morphology of a Genre', *Semeia* 14 (1979), pp. 1-20. This entire volume is helpful as a first approach to the genre apocalypse, and helps, in its attempt to work out a definition and paradigm for one genre, to illuminate questions associated with genre in general. See also the article by H.W. Attridge on 'Greek and Latin Apocalypses', pp. 159-86 in the same volume, which shows the tendency of such apocalypses to be embedded within other host genres.

Hanson, J.S., 'Dreams and Visions in the Greco-Roman World and Early Christianity', *ANRW*, II.23.2, pp. 1395-1427. A helpful introduction to revelatory literature in general, of which *Aseneth* partakes.

Hellholm, David, 'The Problem of Apocalyptic Genre and the Apocalypse of John', in K.H. Richards (ed.), *SBLSP 1982* (Chico, CA: Scholars Press, 1982), pp. 13-64. Hellholm proposes to add the element of 'literary function' to the definition of apocalypse.

Sappington, Thomas J., 'The Factor of Function in Defining Jewish Apocalyptic Literature', *JSP* 12 (1994), pp. 83-123. Distinguishes between literary function and social setting, while it acknowledges that these elements are interrelated. Sappington explores three literary functions in the Jewish apocalypses, and challenges the common view that apocalypses are only implicit in their paraenetic impulse. He argues that function needs to be considered in the understanding of genre.

Yarbro Collins, A. 'Introduction: Early Christian Apocalypses', *Semeia* 36 (1986), pp. 1-11. The SBL Apocalypse group continues their investigation of the genre, building on Semeia 14. In this volume see especially D.E. Aune, 'The Apocalypse of John and the Problem of Genre', pp. 65-96, who discusses inclusive genres in antiquity.

Aseneth and Genre

Bohak, Gideon, *Joseph and Aseneth and the Jewish Temple in Heliopolis* (Early Judaism and
    its Literature, 10; Atlanta: Scholars Press, 1996), pp. 17-18. In this revised disserta-
    tion under the guidance of apocalypse specialist Martha Himmelfarb (*Ascent to
    Heaven in Jewish and Christian Apocalypses* [Oxford: Oxford University Press, 1993]),
    Bohak identifies chs. 14-17 as 'an apocalyptic-revelation scene'.

Burchard, C. 'Joseph et Aséneth: Questions actuelles', in W.C. van Unnik (ed.), *La litter-
    ature juive entre Tenach et Mischna: Quelques problèmes* (RechBib, 9; Leiden: E.J. Brill,
    1974) pp. 77-100. See especially pp. 84-96 for parallels of motifs, structure and plot
    with Latin and Greek romances.

Philonenko, Marc, *Joseph et Aséneth: Introduction, texte critique, traduction et notes* (SPB, 13,
    Leiden: E.J. Brill, 1968). Understands *Aseneth* as a *roman à clef*, encoding Egyptian
    (the goddess Neith), Greek (the sun-god Helios) and Valentinian (Sophia/Logos)
    concepts.

Humphrey, Edith M., *The Ladies and the Cities: Transformation and Apocalyptic Identity in
    Joseph and Aseneth, 4 Ezra, The Apocalypse and The Shepherd of Hermas* (JSPSup, 17;
    Sheffield: Sheffield Academic Press, 1995). See Chapter 2, especially pp. 35-40, for
    Aseneth's affinities with the apocalypse.

Kee, H.C., 'The Socio-Cultural Setting of Joseph and Aseneth', *NTS* 29 (1983), pp.
    394-413. Describes *Aseneth* as an eclectic Hellenistic romance used within Jewish
    circles that had been impressed by mystery cults. See also 'The Socio-Religious
    Setting and Aims of "Joseph and Asenath" ',in G. MacRae (ed.), *SBLSP 1976*
    (Missoula, MT: Scholars Press, 1976), pp. 183-92.

Pervo, R.I., 'Joseph and Asenath and the Greek Novel', in G. MacRae (ed.), *SBLSP
    1976* (Missoula, MT: Scholars Press, 1976), pp. 171-81; and 'Aseneth and her
    Sisters: Women in Jewish Narrative and in Greek Novels', in Amy-Jill Levine (ed.),
    Women Like This; New Perspectives on Jewish Women in the Greco-Roman World
    (Atlanta: Scholars Press, 1991), pp. 145-160. Important comparative studies in rela-
    tion to the classical novel.

West, S. 'Joseph and Asenath: A Neglected Romance', *CQR* 24 (1974), pp. 70-81.
    Considers *Aseneth* a Greek romance with Jewish subject matter.

4. Sociological Issues: Community and Conversion

On the Posing of Questions

The mystique of *Aseneth* has been alluring (and perplexing) not only to
those in search of genre, but also to those concerned with sociological
issues. Indeed, these two realms are not easily separable, because of the
strong connection between function and genre. One may, of course, distinguish between a work's intrinsic or literary 'function' and its usefulness
to the communities that read it. That is, the piece may be considered as
an aesthetic object that indicates how it is to be read by its 'intended' or
'ideal' reader; or, it may be understood as more directly connected to
actual readers (usually a first generation), so that their situation in life is
seen to illuminate its genre and purpose. (Conversely, the book is seen to

illuminate details and world-view of its author and/or readers). Literary convention is always a factor in the analysis, but the accent may be placed upon the work itself (and/or its author) or upon the community that 'owns' it. In any case, genre and sociological context are intertwined. We have seen that a working hypothesis of genre is important to the understanding of any work, even one as complex as *Aseneth*. The importance of recovering a precise sociological location for a text will, however, differ from work to work. Some pieces explicitly invite a discussion of *Sitz im Leben*, since they are overtly tied to community concerns. Others create a literary world removed from that of the author and his/her community, and so obscure to a lesser or greater extent their place of origin. The debate that has raged around *Aseneth* is precisely the question as to whether it is of the first or second type, and if it is of the second sort, how confidently sociological details are to be retrieved.

Arguments concerning the original setting of a work, that is, the supposed shared situation of an author and her/his intended audience, are of various types. Typically in a work of fiction, the first major body of evidence—external data—is limited in usefulness. External evidence might include the claim of a manuscript or a preface to the text regarding its milieu, such as we find in the preface to the non-fictional Sirach. More usually, it takes the form of allusions or citations of the work elsewhere, but this is rare in the case of novels. Internal evidence, then, is the normal point of entry for a piece such as *Aseneth*. Many begin by noting anachronisms, and making linguistic comparisons of various words against our knowledge of their development. Other factors used in such studies are striking parallels—verbal, conceptual, social, historical or cultic—with known communities or other literary products. Throughout the consideration of internal evidence, the question *cui bono* ('for whom would this be useful?') is posed. The scope, motivation and confidence of sociological analysis vary considerably from study to study, and it is helpful to weigh such studies by reference to such questions as 'Why is this question being asked?' 'What and why does the researcher want to know?' and 'How precise an answer is being sought?'

Of immense help in clarifying issues surrounding socio-historical setting and purpose is the paper 'From Text to Context: The Social Matrix of *Joseph and Aseneth*' (*SBLSP 1996* [Atlanta, GA: Scholars Press, 1996], pp. 285-302), recently offered by Randall Chesnutt to the Society of Biblical Literature's Pseudepigrapha group. There, he 'clears the air' by grouping previous proposals into two groups—a history-of-religions approach, which depends upon perceived parallels between ideas and practices found in *Aseneth* and in the religious world of late antiquity; and a literary-historical approach, which links the plot, characters and language of *Aseneth* to actual events in (especially Egyptian) Jewish history. His division suggests two major tendencies, while there are cases of overlap, where the arguments for religion and historical event come together. However, the discussion remains extremely valuable, as Chesnutt demonstrates from *Aseneth* the cautions of Sandmel's 1962 essay, 'Parallelomania' (*JBL* 81 [1962] pp. 1-13): *one must distinguish between correlation and cause, between similarity and dependence!*

History of Religion Parallels

Unfortunately, enthusiasm for sociological mirror-reading has banished this warning from the memories of many researchers. (For all the following, see 'Further Reading', pp. 62-63). Kuhn and Delcor seized upon the blessed meal imagery, and Beckwith upon an implicit view of calendar; all three argued for an Essene (or more specifically Therapeutic) origin. Kilpatrick began from the same bread and wine imagery, suggesting that concepts in *Aseneth* and the New Testament each developed separately from an archetypal, but now unknown, Jewish meal; Philonenko saw the same passages as indicative of a Jewish mystery cult. M. de Goeij and Priesbatch highlighted the mystic relationship between Joseph and Aseneth, and so detected a second-century Valentinian Gnostic setting. Kee and Kraemer have also called attention to the mystic atmosphere, and have set *Aseneth* alongside the practices of merkavah mysticism (Kraemer also sees parallels with neo-Platonism, adjuration and magic). To those who read between the lines of *Aseneth* in order to find intimations of characteristic ideas or cultic practices, impertinent questions must be directed. Where is the strong eschatological impulse of the Qumran community? Where is the ascetic drive of the Therapeutae, given the erotic nature of the story and the comfortable life of its protagonists? Where is there an actual cultic meal in the book, parallel to the mystery cults, as distinct from mere language? Where is the disdain for matter commonly shown by Gnostic thinkers or even their general view of the cosmos? Where are the *specific* preparatory practices and rewards of those merkavah mystics who 'went down' to the chariot? Where is there evidence of theurgic manipulation of the gods in the demeanour of the humble Aseneth?

In each of these proposals, the parallels adduced are outweighed by significant omissions and differences. Thus, while not precluding the possibility of influences from any or several of the sectarian communities to which these scholars appeal, it is wise to remain cautious about sociological construction based upon the internal evidence of a fictional work. The genre of *Aseneth* renders it stubbornly resistant to such analysis; even anachronisms are not always helpful in this regard, since novels abound in archaisms, and since the textual transmission of the apocryphon has been so very complex. For example, it is too simple to consider the Latin word *solarion* in the short recension (7.2 *Aseneth* [*P*]) as a telltale sign of Roman origins, or to adduce the term *satrapēs* (1.6; 1.9*P*) as evidence for an ancient Persian dating. In the first case, the Latin word may have been added to a later manuscript tradition, and in the second, we find numerous archaizing uses of this term for rulers in Greek novels. The very number of proposals predicated upon the 'holy meal' language suggests the precariousness of confident assignation to specific cults.

Encoded Events in the Narrative

Even more unlikely are suggestions as to encoded historical details and events. Sänger (*Antikes Judentum und die Mysterien: Religionsgeschichtliche Untersuchungen zu Joseph und Aseneth* [WUNT, 2.5; Tübingen: J.C.B. Mohr (Paul Siebeck), 1980]), while steadfastly avoiding the parallelomania typical of history-of-religions approaches, has read the details of *Aseneth* as indicative of tensions between Alexandrian Jews and anti-Judaic Gentiles, faithful Jews and opportunistic Jewish collaborators, in first-century Egypt. In this reading the second story is particularly important, within which each group—Pharaoh and Pentephres, Pharaoh's son and his men, the sons of Leah, the sons of Bilhah and Zilpah—represents a player in the historical scene. Thus, the story-line, in introducing Pharaoh's son, intends to evoke the anti-Jewish sentiments that led to outright persecution in 38 CE. On the other hand, Bohak (*Joseph and Aseneth*) highlights the *friendly* relations between Pharaoh and Joseph, and draws a parallel with the alliance between the Oniad settlement in Heliopolis and the Ptolemaic rulers in second-century BCE Egypt. However, the fictional character of *Aseneth* conspires against such analyses—tensions and interrelationships are the stuff of good stories; the Genesis point of departure requires the friendship of Pharaoh and Joseph.

A promising *entreé* may be suspected where the story-line seems out of line with the book's explicit statements about social realities. For example, *Aseneth* is a true 'comedy', in that the obstacles at the onset of the plot are overcome, so that the protagonist is integrated into her fictive society. However, the obstacles presented within this story do not include parental or societal objection to conversion, which would indeed have made for an intriguing romance. Rather, it is Aseneth's own idolatry, pride and 'misandrist' tendencies that threaten to thwart a marriage *desired* by Pentephres and indeed foreseen by heaven itself. Further, Pentephres and his wife are delighted by the fortunes of their daughter, and the betrothal of her to Joseph is sealed by a family meal; Pharaoh himself performs the ceremony. In contrast to the plot line, Aseneth's prayer of confession stresses her rejection by her native community as a result of conversion. This trope is particularly highlighted in the long recension, where it frames her three penitential discourses, occurring at the beginning of the first lament and at the conclusion of the final prayer (11.2-6//12.12). It might seem obvious that these laments about societal exclusion mirror tensions known intimately to the author and the intended readers. Why else include elements that are in dissonance with the actual story? However, it is also possible that the 'rejection' motif is a traditional one, typical of conversion stories, at home within the poetic language of prayer, and intended to bolster Aseneth's status, despite its lack of connection with the outer story. The exclusion trope, then, tells us something about general fears and possibilities concerning the persecution of converts to Judaism in antiquity, but may not tell us anything about the author's particular experience. Thus, we may speculate about which communities may have sympathized with the dangers of conversion, but must not equate utility or resonance with historical origin.

Sociological Studies and *Aseneth*

Burchard tells the reader that in seeking to locate *Aseneth* within Judaism, 'it is easier to say what it is not', but then suggests that it 'may be more representative of Greek-speaking Judaism than we have previously imagined' (*OTP*, II, p. 194). In the case of a fictive work, written in a period that is relatively obscure, the search for a specific *Sitz im Leben*, whether aimed at the retrieval of a specific cult, or at the knowledge of specific historical events in a given place, is fraught with difficulty. Of more use are the cautious studies of sociologists who turn to *Aseneth* to understand general aspects of communities in antiquity. Studies of conversion and community dynamics that use *Aseneth* as a departure point are intriguing. The analysis of Aseneth's progress from the perspective of initiation rites *in general* seems far more helpful than an appeal to particular cult practices. Rees Conrad Douglas ('Liminality and Conversion in Joseph and

Aseneth', *JSP* 3 [1988], pp. 1-42) has used the anthropological studies of others (see references to Victor W. Turner and B. Lincoln in 'Further Reading' pp. 62-63) in his study of the motifs of separation, liminality, transformation and aggregation in *Aseneth*. He considers the emerging identity of Aseneth as a female initiate, and notes the work's stress upon maintaining and overcoming boundaries—that is, its concern for group identity. The strength of this study is its serious consideration of Aseneth's transformation and identity; its weakness lies in the assumption that the apocryphon is concerned with *women's* integration, when Aseneth is clearly a symbolic figure.

The work of Randall Chesnutt (*From Death*) probes even more deeply into the sociology of conversion, wisely concluding that *Aseneth* is not a missionary work, but a work intended to buttress the status of converts within the Jewish (Egyptian?) community. He gives attention to the narrative elements of *Aseneth*, especially to the areas of tension, such as between Jew and gentile, and between Jew and Jew. In his reading (see also Philonenko and Sänger), Aseneth's own actions provide the turning point of the piece, and the epiphanic passage is merely confirmatory of a conversion that has already been effected by Aseneth's repudiation of idolatry (*From Death*, p. 137). We might wonder at this point whether emphasis upon the sociology of conversion has prevented this writer from heeding the structural and verbal cues given in the apocryphon itself. That is, he is concerned to examine Aseneth's conversion in relation to contemporary paradigms, and so may be predisposed to see her actions as the decisive ones, rather than focusing upon the divine initiative that is evident throughout *Aseneth*.

It might be worthwhile considering at this point whether religious conversion by its very nature is a drama that demands a protracted turning point: change in the attitudes and actions of the convert; acceptance and/or transformation by the deity; recognition by and integration into new community. (The stages of separation, liminality and aggregation may be instructive here!) It might, then, be ill-conceived to seek one distinct *peripeteia* (turning point), but to expect a process, which is indeed what the story relates. At every stage, however, divine agency is in view. Aseneth changes as a result of a quasi-epiphanic vision of Joseph, and in response to his threefold prayer on her behalf. (See the earlier discussion on p. 24 of the triadic formulae and its contribution to the narrative integrity of the story.) She takes courage to pray because of what she has heard about the Hebrew God. Her repentance is sincere, but the transformation is by no means complete until she has been visited by a divine messenger, himself a great mystery. Even her integration into Hebrew society is catalysed by the visit of a messenger to Joseph, and by Joseph's recognition of her transformation at God's hands. We will investigate the structure of *Aseneth* in the next chapter, but will at this point simply consider an oracle concerning the timing of her acceptance. If indeed a choice is to be made concerning the definitive act by which Aseneth is changed, then these (from the longer text) are the operative words:

> Behold *from today* you will be renewed and formed anew and made alive again, and you will eat blessed bread of life and drink a blessed cup of immortality and anoint yourself with blessed ointment of incorruptibility. Courage, Aseneth, chaste virgin. Behold I have given you *today* to Joseph for a bride, and he himself will be your bridegroom forever and ever (15.5-6).

The mysterious Visitor utters a performative word, calling the new Aseneth into being. This utterance is in no way mitigated by what the Visitor has already told her: that her name 'was written' (15.4) in God's book as the first of all. The aorist tense in 15.4 does not refer to God's *response* to Aseneth's repentance, but to his eternal will for the mother of converts. In the heavenly book, Aseneth's name is recorded eternally; in the human story, she is accepted and given her new status at the word of the divine messenger.

While we might thus question whether Chesnutt's accent upon the human elements of conversion adequately captures the world-view of this epiphanic novel, his approach to sociological questions remains an excellent model. He steadfastly opposes the undisciplined drawing of parallels while tuning a sensitive ear to the inner dynamics of *Aseneth*—those themes and phrases that permeate its narrative and so suggest the live issues of its author and readership. His analysis demonstrates no close connection between the book and the formal or ritualistic initiating features of any one sect. Rather, the 'sociological dimensions' of conversion and of Jewish life in a Gentile world are reflected. Constant reference to actions and attitudes that 'befit one who worships God' suggest the dilemma of maintaining faith in a foreign environment; Joseph's discrete meal and gracious refusal of intimacy with Aseneth may well serve as a model; discord between the patriarchs, foreshadowed in the 'apocalypse' and played out in the second narrative, seem too pointed for a mere plot device; the emphasis upon benevolence towards outsiders and forgiveness of enemies has a moralistic ring, and is frequently accompanied by the 'it befits' refrain.

The least that can be deduced from such data is that the author is well aware of the social and religious tensions associated with maintaining fidelity in a plural society. This emphasis on intramural issues also means that *Aseneth* is directed to those *within* the faithful community (either by birth or by integration), rather than intended as a missionary tract. In this regard note that the tale is content to naturalize Aseneth without going on to speak of the conversion of her family or of Pharaoh and those in his world: peaceful coexistence rather than vigorous proselytism is the ideal. However, these general concerns for community identity do not easily suggest a specific milieu. The absence of explicit reference to ablution, to specific food laws, to circumcision and to sacrifice has been seen by some as problematic for a Jewish milieu. (Circumcision and sacrifice are less critical, considering the subject matter of the novel—a woman's conversion prior to the time of the Temple).

Certainly the text's silence on these matters rendered the book more useful in its Christian transmission, but the omissions do not militate against a Jewish context. Yet some have coupled this relaxed attitude towards distinctive features of Judaism with the author's penchant for wisdom motifs, mystical knowledge, and food-wine-ointment imagery, seeking an explanation elsewhere. Others have noted that our growing knowledge of formative Judaism brings surprises, and that a firm division between mainline and sectarian Judaism is anachronistic. This fluidity, however, is less helpful as a governing principle if the critic assumes, with Ross Kraemer, that the novel was written at a later time, since by the late second and early third centuries, the distinguishing features of rabbinic Judaism and Christianity were well in place. The increasing crystallization of these two religions may well have rendered the novel suspect in one of the mainstreams: *Aseneth*'s lack of transmission (or aborted transmission) in the later Jewish milieu may mean that the book was rejected by later 'orthodoxy'.

Kraemer, however, extends the period of social fluidity well into the third and fourth centuries, and highlights the transformative and mystical elements of *Aseneth*. While she avoids the pitfalls of a specific social hypothesis in this way, some may want to question her construal of social life and her reading of the apocryphon. In response to *Aseneth*'s mystique, she draws general parallels with practices that are said to have been prevalent in late antiquity among varied groups, Jewish or otherwise. In particular, she argues that parallels between *Aseneth* and theurgical practices show the book to be not so much about conversion *per se* but about the adjuration of an angel by a woman (*When Aseneth*, p. 90). Kraemer adduces parallels to the Greek Magical Papyri and the Jewish *Sepher ha-Razim*. (On these roughly contemporary—third and fourth century?—works, see 'Further Reading' pp. 62-63). But the practices of fasting, mourning, purification, change of location and clothes, and petition are found in a variety of visionary and apocalyptic writings of earlier times. Missing from *Aseneth* are the more intricate prescriptions found in either the magic papyri or the Hebrew Book of Mysteries: the necessary presence of a mystagogue, the use of ivy for covering, or nakedness, the covering of the eyes, the gathering of animals or natural products, and above all, the repetitive pronouncement of secret names. The few *particular* parallels adduced—the seclusion in a tower, the throwing of food to the dogs—make sense within the narrative itself, and are not introduced as a 'technique' to force God's hand. Never is there a sense in the text that Aseneth's behaviour or speech *compels* a visit by a figure from heaven. Divine initiative is so underscored that Aseneth tentatively muses, in language reminiscent of Mordecai, Tobit and the penitent David (whose petition is not granted!): 'Who knows, [maybe] he will see my humiliation and have mercy on me' (11.12; cf. Est. 4.14; Tob. 13.6; 2 Sam. 12.22). The most glaring omission is that in *Aseneth* there is no actual adjuration or command or a recitation of the divine Name(s). Especially in the longer version, this procedure is explicitly feared by Aseneth, who doubts that she should name his 'terrible holy name' (11.17). When she does, the naming is in no way incantatory, nor lengthy, but confined to the formula 'Lord God of the ages' (12.1), a title that is abbreviated to 'Lord' in all the ensuing petitions. Her reverence for the name seems to be one common to the religious tradition, and not a reaction against the excesses of some mystical practices.

Kraemer remarks that the longer version makes the adjurative associations explicit, in the same way that it intensifies its biblical intertexts. While the similarities she lists are intriguing, and may indicate an understanding of general mysticism, the long text also thoroughly fences off any suggestion that the God of Jacob can be controlled. Any theurgic practice is carefully circumscribed. Of particular interest are Kraemer's references to the chariot and to Helios in the Greek papyri and the *Sepher ha-Razim*, an obvious point of contact with the sun-like Visitor, the divine Joseph and divinely transformed Aseneth. However, such thematic similarities do not warrant a direct relationship.

Kraemer moves on from her discussion of magical texts to the Hebrew texts termed *hekhalot* (literally, 'palaces'), which are associated with merkavah mysticism. The investigation of these sources is warranted by *Aseneth*'s chariot imagery and pervasive theme of transformation, and has been conducted in a more tentative way by Howard Kee ('Socio-cultural Setting'. Kee's preliminary work has not been convincing to many, since here again the details—chariot epiphany, changes of clothing, hymnic response to revelation, transformation into quasi-angelic appearance, theme of glory and trials following a revelation— may all be found in other literature.

Kraemer has sought to be at once more thorough and more cautious: she suggests that 'the two (*Aseneth* and the *hekhalot*) might...be located much closer in time, space and community' than Kee thought, while admitting it 'is almost impossible to establish...whether there is any direct relationship between the two' (*When Aseneth*, n. 2 versus n. 5, p. 139). In Kraemer's study, as in Kee's, the parallels are not precise. Aseneth herself does not ascend (or, to use the rabbinic language, 'descend') to the throne or chariot of God in order to be transformed; nor does she actually call down a divine being; nor, like the adept in the 'Prince of the Torah' traditions, does she seize Torah through mystical means. Her mediated vision and knowledge of eternal things, her transformation and her reception of wisdom and the honeycomb (cf. Torah) are divine gifts, and not humanly engineered. Imagery, architecture, language, and prayer-forms of *Aseneth* yield some similarities to the *hekhalot* texts (more similarities, it would seem, than to the adjuration spells cited earlier). However, in the overall atmosphere there is an enormous gap. We find here no journeys to the heavenly worlds, and few if any theurgic elements (*pace* Kraemer), such as the invoking of the divine Name, the use of special objects and the intricate bodily preliminaries to visions which are prescribed in the *hekhalot* texts (cf. *Hekhaloth Zutreti* 407-409; *Rabbati* 81, 204-251; and *Ma'aseh Merkabah* 544-555.) Are such practices even discouraged in the narrative? It is hard to be sure. Of great import to Kraemer is the mysterious Visitor, this curious *Anthrōpos* (Human Being), and his affinities to the later known figure 'Metatron' (the one beside/with the throne), or 'Second Power' seen in the heavens and named by merkavah mystics. But a major point in our novel's 'apocalypse' is that this figure is neither named nor praised by Aseneth.

Balancing Aspects of *Aseneth*

The shortfalls experienced by Kee and Kraemer in connecting *Aseneth* with the merkavah texts and practices render the cautions of Burchard (*OTP*, II, p. 191 n. 72) and Chesnutt (*From Death*, pp. 211-14) pertinent. On the other hand, there is a real danger of ignoring the nuances of *Aseneth* if its novelistic and biblical tendencies are so stressed that its mystical propensities are obscured. With Kraemer and Kee, but against Chesnutt and Burchard, I see in *Aseneth* a major distinctive feature of merkavah mysticism—the centrality of a revelatory experience as constitutive of transformation. This is not to say that the author or readers of *Aseneth* expected to undergo mystical experiences or literal physical transformation, as does their heroine—Aseneth is a fictive character, though in some sense paradigmatic. Moreover, other important elements, including strict adherence to the prescriptions of Torah, are missing from the apocryphon. It is thus apparent that we cannot appeal to the zenith of this Jewish mystical movement in antiquity. Far from reinforcing a third- to fourth-century date for *Aseneth*, the imperfectness of comparisons with merkavah texts suggests a time much earlier. Unfortunately, our understanding of mystical Judaism at the turn of the eras is as shady as our certainty about the origins of this apocryphon.

Thus, our provisional placing of this book, and our search for its original and ongoing functions should not stress its romantic and commonplace religious nature to the exclusion of its esoteric dimension. It is difficult to deny that *Aseneth* has been in some way informed by mystical traditions, given its constant emphasis upon spiritual knowledge and transformation. Certainly the novel is not in the centre of a full-blown tradition such as later merkavah mysticism. Chesnutt is correct that many of the parallels drawn with the merkavah mystics are to be found in the Hebrew bible or other groups/bodies of literature besides the *hekhalot* texts. On the other hand, it may be significant that we have a grouping or configuration of features in *Aseneth* and not the odd casual likeness. In particular, the significance of Aseneth's angelic revelation is not to be underplayed. The next chapter will argue that both the implicit polemic and the literary structure of the book stress the epiphany, with all it disclosure and its mystery, as the centre of Aseneth's conversion. Kee and, it would seem, Kraemer as well, may have played their hand too confidently in adducing merkavah parallels; yet I cannot agree with Chesnutt that the apocalypse section is merely 'subsidiary to Aseneth's conversion' (*From Death*, p. 213).

Aseneth is, then, no *hekhalot* text. However, those who reject the assessments of Kee and Kraemer must still contend with the piece's enigmatic curiosities. A.F. Segal, for example, compares *Aseneth* with *b. Šab.* 17b. In his analysis he confirms Chesnutt's opinion that the 'puzzling objects of Aseneth's rites [i.e. bread, cup and anointing] are apparently symbolic of Jewish life in general, rather than representative of a specific

2. *Issues in Interpretation* 59

conversion ritual' ('Conversion and Messianism: Outline for New Approach', in J.H. Charlesworth [ed.], *The Messiah: Developments in Earliest Judaism and Christianity* [Minneapolis: Fortress Press, 1992], pp. 296-340 [311]). His views are shared by Burchard (*OTP*, p. 212 n. i) and will be buttressed by a forthcoming article of Chesnutt, 'The Dead Sea Scrolls and the Meal Formula in *Joseph and Aseneth*: From Qumran Fever to Qumran Light', in vol. IV of J.H. Charlesworth (ed.), *The Bible and the Dead Sea Scrolls: The Jubilee Publication* (Berkley, CA: BIBAL Press, forthcoming). Chesnutt here carefully examines the triadic formula of bread, drink and ointment in terms of Qumranian and Talmudic parallels, concluding that no actual ritual can be discerned in the *Aseneth* triad; rather, the formula is 'expressive of the whole Jewish way of life' in which the faithful sought to maintain purity in these daily realities of life, that is, food, drink and oil. (See especially the two concluding paragraphs to his article.) However, despite the careful work of Segal and Chesnutt, we continue to puzzle over the extravagant language used in the 'meal' dyad or triad: 'blessed bread of life, blessed cup of *immortality*, [blessed unction of *incorruptibility*]' (c.f. 8.9; 15.5; 16.16). Does a common Jewish fear of corrupt Gentile staples, and the prospect of ordinary Jewish eating and anointing account sufficiently for this recurrent formula? What are we to make of its connection with the 'food of the angels' symbolized by the mysterious honeycomb, and of Aseneth's assertion that she has been fed in this way and so transformed (19.5)? It is also curious that in every place where the triad is abridged to a double formula, the speaker goes on to speak about how Aseneth has been transformed, added to Israel, or made the bride of Joseph—the implication is that the anointing is, at least in its first instance, connected with her transfer of allegiance.

Certainly, we have no parallel more exact than that of the Christian Eucharist and Chrismation, and yet the book is lacking in unambiguously specific Christian references. The paucity of evidence concerning Judaisms at the turn of the eras (in which earliest 'Christianity' is to be situated), and our access to this time through mostly later texts, adds to our difficulty in making sense of such phrases, and may continue to lead some, such as Ross Kraemer, to decide for a later date for our piece. It is becoming clearer that several concepts that we normally associate with Christianity were more broadly acceptable in this time of formation—for example, evidence for belief in 'two powers' in heaven, a mystical teaching later proscribed by the rabbis (cf. A.F. Segal, 'Heavenly Ascent in Hellenistic Judaism, Early Christianity and their Environment', *ANRW*, II.23.2, especially pp. 1352-68; *idem*, *Two*

Powers in Heaven: Rabbinic Reports about Christianity and Gnosticism
[Leiden: E.J. Brill, 1977]). Such fluidity between turn of the era
Judaisms (which included formative Christianity) may possibly apply to
liturgical language that we now know only in the Christian context.

For now we may suspect with reason that *Aseneth* has been informed
by some of the mystical traditions that fed into traditions which we have
documented only at a later time—traditions situated in Christian and/or
in Jewish milieus. That we do not have direct access to the earliest traditions means that anomalies and puzzles will continue to disturb the ana-
lyst—see, for example, Ross Kraemer's worry over the seeming
contradiction in the longer version, where the Visitor is identified in
some sense with God, yet Aseneth may not worship him (*When Aseneth*,
p. 127). Is the attitude to the Visitor indicative of the reverence afforded
quasi-divine beings like Metatron, or opposed to such worship?
Instructive here may be a similar, but not identical, ambiguity in Paul's
letters. He himself experienced mystical visions (2 Cor. 12), and used
language derived from Ezekiel (perhaps in consonance with a proto-
merkavah tradition) in order to describe the Christian life and standing—
light versus dark, life from death, transformation into the image,
beholding 'the light of the knowledge of the glory of God' (cf. Ezek.
1.18). Yet it is certain that he did not expect members of his flock to
approximate his own visual enlightenment, and may even have warned
them against seeking such experiences. (See my analysis, 'Why Bring the
Word Down?—the Rhetoric of Demonstration and Disclosure in
Romans 9.30–10.21', in S. Soderlund and N.T. Wright [eds.], *Paul's
Letter to the Romans and the People of God* [Festschrift Gordon Fee; Grand
Rapids: Eerdmans, 1999], pp. 129-48.) It is evident that writers may use
language and even concepts from a certain milieu that is recognized by
their readers, without endorsing the whole framework of ideas or practices associated with them, and sometimes with the intent of correcting
or adding nuances to these. Such points of contact do not mean that the
author and ideal reader belonged to such a group, or even commended
mystical practices to others. Kraemer herself suggests that *Aseneth* may
reflect a world-view that provided 'a deliberate counterpart' to the
hekhalot traditions (*When Aseneth*, p. 138) in that humans considered
themselves to have an angelic (already transformed) identity yet led ordinary lives within families. This would be possible if *Aseneth* were written
at a time when *hekhalot* texts could be known: it seems more likely that
the novel is informed by and sometimes reacts against a less developed or
differently construed mystical tradition from an earlier period. We are at

every turn hampered by the limits of mirror-reading, especially when faced with a fictive text and a relatively obscure religious milieu. The latter constriction may be gradually loosened by our increased access to the written products of the Second Temple Period and the time immediately following it; the fictional genre of *Aseneth* will always mean that our reconstructions remain provisional.

What is quite clear, however, is that we can appreciate works like Aseneth without a perfect access to their setting, and with only provisional reconstructions of the communities that read the novel. The argument for a very particular milieu may sometimes work against the appreciation of *Aseneth*'s ongoing vitality. Bohak, for example, concentrates upon the honeycomb episode (16.17–17.2) and the setting of an Oniad alternate Temple cult to such an extent that this mystery is declared to be 'what Joseph and Aseneth originally was all about' (*Joseph and Aseneth*, p. 106). But even if Bohak's hypothesis were to be fully confirmed, our considerations of genre forbid that we see in *Aseneth* simply a hidden apology for an alternate temple. That the book lived on, sometimes in a version that uncritically abridged the honeycomb and bee vision demonstrates that is not all about one single thing. Moreover, even if some details of the apocalypse are soluble by reference to literary, historical and sociological analysis, there remains in Aseneth (over against other merely allegorical apocalypses, for example. 'The Animal Apocalypse' of *1 Enoch* 85–90) an undivulged innermost mystery—the name of the heavenly Visitor. Bohak may yet convince the scholarly community that *Aseneth* has an argumentative dimension that uses revelation to authenticate a cult. This will not mean that the work ceases to touch the nerves of mystical desire, religious awe, ethics and sheer entertainment. Any 'solution' that reduces the piece, or cuts it down to one size has forgotten its unusual genre and its staying power throughout centuries of diverse communities.

This, then, is a plea that the search for milieu or the use of *Aseneth* to clarify sociological issues does not become a process that explains *away* the mystery of this piece. It is easy in retrospect to see how past scholars have done just this, through unacknowledged assumptions and pursuits peculiar to their own culture. Not so very long ago, *Aseneth* was studied patronizingly as a prime example of the decadent and artificial literature of the 'Second Sophistic' period (i.e. the revival of Greek philosophy and culture in the imperial period, in its heyday during the second century CE). That assessment is now understood more as a window into tastes of the last century than as an adequate description of the varied aspect of popular romances (Pervo, *Profit with Delight*, pp. 87-90). Historical criticism and sociological study can be similarly tyrannical: often reading behind the lines or between the lines is confused for a reading of the lines. This is all the more true of studies that are directly informed by ideological concerns, as in the subsection of sociological analysis to which we now turn—the consideration of *Aseneth* from a feminist perspective.

Further Reading

The Peril of Parallels

Buchard, C., 'Joseph and Aseneth', in J.H. Charlesworth (ed.), *The Old Testament Pseudepigrapha*, II (2 vols.; Garden City, NY: Doubleday, 1983-85), pp. 177-247.

Chesnutt, Randall D., 'From Text to Context', in *SBLSP 1996* (Atlanta, GA: Scholars Press, 1996), pp. 285-302. Cites numerous past excesses in the attempt to find religious or historical clues in Aseneth. 'The Dead Sea Scrolls and the Meal Formula in Joseph and Aseneth: From Qumran Fever to Qumran Light': in-depth article soon to be published by J.H. Charlesworth in vol. IV of the collection of essays from the symposium *Biblical Theology and the Dead Sea Scrolls: The Jubilee Publication* (Berkeley, CA: BIBAL Press, forthcoming).

Sandmel, S., 'Parallelomania', *JBL* 81 (1962), pp. 1-13.

Sociological Studies of *Aseneth*

Beckwith, R.T., 'The Solar Calendar of *Joseph and Aseneth*: A Suggestion', *JSJ* 15 (1984), pp. 90-110. An Essene view of *Aseneth*, stressing eschatology.

Bohak, Gideon, *Joseph and Aseneth and the Jewish Temple in Heliopolis* (Early Judaism and its Literature, 10; Atlanta: Scholars Press, 1996). Identifies the 'honeycomb episode' as an apocalyptic revelation, and interprets the whole of *Aseneth* as a piece justifying the alternate Heliopolitan temple.

Chesnutt, Randall, *From Death to Life: Conversion in Joseph and Aseneth* (JSPSup, 16; Sheffield: Sheffield Academic Press, 1995). Conversion in *Aseneth*, concise summary of other views.

Delcor, M., 'Un roman d'amour d'origine thérapeute: Le Livre de Joseph et Asénath', *BLE* 63 (1962), pp. 3-27. Defends a Therapeutic context.

Douglas, Rees Conrad, 'Liminality and Conversion in Joseph and Aseneth', *JSP* 3 (1988), pp. 1-42. Douglas draws on A. van Gennep, *The Rites of Passage* (ET M.B. Vizedom and G.L. Coffee; Chicago: University of Chicago Press, 1960); Victor W. Turner, 'Betwixt and Between: The Liminal Period in *Rites de Passage*', in *Forest of Symbols* (Ithaca, NY: Cornell University Press, 1967), pp. 93-11; and B. Lincoln, *Emerging from the Chrysalis: Studies in Rituals of Women's Initiation* (London: Routledge & Kegan Paul, 1966).

Goeij, M. de, *Jozef en Aseneth: Apokalyps van Baruch* (De Pseudepigraphen, 2; Kampen: Kok, 1981). A Dutch translation and introduction, arguing for an early Valentinian context.

Kee, H.C. 'The Socio-Cultural Setting of Joseph and Aseneth', *NTS* 29 (1983), pp. 394-413, and 'The Socio-Religious Setting and Aims of "Joseph and Asenath"', in G. MacRae (ed.), *SBLSP 1976* (Missoula, MT: Scholars Press, 1976), pp. 183-92. *Aseneth* and merkavah.

Kilpatrick, G.D., 'The Last Supper', *ExpTim* 64 (1952), pp. 4-8. Attempts to demonstrate the relevance of *Aseneth* to Christian rites.

Kraemer, Ross Shepard, *When Aseneth Met Joseph: A Late Antique Tale of the Biblical Patriarch
and his Egyptian Wife, Reconsidered* (New York: Oxford University Press, 1998).
Adduces various parallels, stressing the practices of adjuration in late antiquity.

Kuhn, K.G., 'The Lord's Supper and the Communal Meal at Qumran', in K. Stendahl (ed.),
The Scrolls and the New Testament (New York: Harper & Brothers., 1957), pp. 65-93.

Pervo, R.I., *Profit with Delight: The Literary Genre of the Acts of the Apostles* (Philadelphia:
Fortress Press, 1987).

Philonenko, Marc, *Joseph et Aséneth: Introduction, texte critique, traduction et notes* (SPB, 13;
Leiden: E.J. Brill, 1968). *Aseneth* and Jewish mystery cults.

Priesbatch, H., *Die Josephsgeschichte in der Weltliteratur* (Breslau: np., 1937). A second-
century Valentinian Gnostic setting for *Aseneth*.

Sänger, D., 'Erwägungen zur historischen Einordnung und zur Datierung von "Joseph
und Aseneth" ', *ZNW* 76 (1985), pp. 86-106. Encoded historical details of
Alexandria in *Aseneth*.

Sänger, D., *Antikes Judentum und die Mysterien: Religionsgeschichtliche Untersuchungen zu
Joseph und Aseneth* (WUNT, 2.5; Tübingen: J.C.B. Mohr [Paul Siebeck], 1980).
Argues that *Aseneth* was not intended as missionary literature for Gentiles, and that a
cultic meal is encoded in the mystical language, although this is diffficult to retrieve.

Apocalypses, Magic and Mysticism (Primary and Secondary Sources)

Betz, Hans Dieter (ed.), *The Greek Magical Papyri in Translation, Including the Demotic Spells*
(Chicago: University of Chicago Press, 1986). Accessible translation of the papyri.

Gruenwald, Ithamar, *Apocalyptic and Merkavah Mysticism* (Leiden: E.J. Brill, 1980).

Halperin, David J., *The Faces of the Chariot: Early Jewish Responses to Ezekiel's Vision*
(Tübingen: J.C.B. Mohr [Paul Siebeck], 1988).

Humphrey, E.M., 'Why Bring the Word Down?—the Rhetoric of Demonstration and
Disclosure in Romans 9.30-1021', in S. Soderlund and N.T. Wright (eds.), *Paul's
Letter to the Romans and the People of God* (Festschrift Gordon Fee; Grand Rapids:
Eerdmans, 1999), pp. 129-48.

Morgan, Michael, *Sepher ha-Razim: The Book of the Mysteries* (Chico, CA: Scholars Press,
1983). A helpful English translation of the Hebrew text.

Schäfer, Peter, *Synopse zur Hekhalot-Literatur in Zusammenarbeit mit Margarete Schlüter und
Hans Georg von Mutius: Herausgegeben von Peter Schäfer* (Texte und Studien zum
Antiken Judentum, 2; Tübingen: J.C.B. Mohr [Paul Siebeck], 1981). A helpful syn-
opsis of the merkavah material, some of which is translated into English in Halperin,
Faces of the Chariot.

Scholem, Gershom, *Major Trends in Jewish Mysticism* (repr.; New York: Schocken Books,
3rd edn, 1960 [1954]).

Segal, Alan, *Paul the Convert: The Apostolate and Apostasy of Saul the Pharisee* (New Haven:
Yale University Press, 1990).

—'Heavenly Ascent in Hellenistic Judaism, Early Christianity and their Environment',
ANRW, II.23.2, pp. 1333-94.

—'Conversion and Messianism: Outline for a New Approach', in J.H Charlesworth
(ed.), *The Messiah: Developments in Earliest Judaism and Christianity* (Minneapolis:
Fortress Press, 1992), pp. 298-340 (311).

—*Two Powers in Heaven: Rabbinic Reports about Christianity and Gnosticism* (Leiden: E.J.
Brill, 1977).

5. Feminist Readings

What to do with Aseneth? This is the recurring question that emerges for feminist and pro-feminist readings of this book, and one that is complicated by the lack of consensus regarding text, genre, 'purpose' and provenance. In the early years of *Aseneth*'s 'second début' (the mid-1980s) writers were happy to point out that the book had been traditionally misnamed, since it has but one major protagonist and not two. As a result, there were suggestions for a reversion to titles, such as Batiffol, *Prière d'Aséneth*, and Kohler, *Life and Confession...of Asenath* (*JewEnc*, II), or for a renaming as (simply) *Aseneth*. Christopher Burchard (*OTP*, II, p. 181), in introducing the apocryphon to a larger English-reading audience, retained the 'traditional' title of *Joseph and Aseneth*, while remarking that *Aseneth*, coupled with an indication of genre (*History of...*, *Book of...*) may have been its earlier designation. In fact, the double name, beginning with the male of a couple, seems to have come into common use by analogy with the Greek and Roman romances (cf. *Chaireas and Callirhoe*, *Daphnis and Chloe*). I myself use the short designation *Aseneth* here, as in an earlier study (*The Ladies*), mostly for convenience, but also in reaction to the contemporary pro-liferation of coded short forms (*JosAsen*, *JBap*, *GThom...*), and out of respect for the character of the book. (*Joseph* would never have done!)

The new titles, in their freshness, breathed intimations of the novel's usefulness for feminist studies. That path has been, not surprisingly, pursued by more than a few, but with an alarming disparity of method, analysis and conclusion. The character of Aseneth is sometimes depicted as a (*mutatis mutandis*) 'feminist' model for early readers, or as a clue to female authorship; alternately, she is seen as a traditionally sub-ordinate character who exemplifies the misogyny of her day, and who encodes traits desirable only to her male author and androcentric read-ership. Several critics provide a more nuanced presentation, cognisant of the textual difficulties, and cautious in their movement towards social analysis. Their wisdom is, it seems, warranted by this enigmatic piece. With this variation of views in mind, let us move on to look at the issues that are engaging critics today.

The Title, and Aseneth as the Central Figure

We can isolate at least four connected concerns in feminist approaches to this book: the prominence of Aseneth as heroine and a corresponding title for the piece; the character of the different versions of *Aseneth* as feminist or patriarchal; Aseneth's status or position in the book as related to social realities of the time; and the plausibility of female authorship of *Aseneth*. We begin with the centrality of the heroine, and the question of a title. The objection to the most usual designation *Joseph **and Aseneth*** has been that this title places the character who occupies centre-stage in a secondary and affiliated position. Even such scholars as Chesnutt, who retain the title, acquiesce: 'Aseneth so dominates the apocryphon...that the title now commonly used...must be judged a misnomer' ('Revelatory Experiences Attributed to Biblical Women', in Amy-Jill Levine [ed.], *'Women Like This': New Perspectives on Jewish Women in the Greco-Roman World* [Atlanta: Scholars Press, 1991], pp. 107-25 [111]). Others argue strongly that the persisting double title does a disservice to the piece, and skews its reading, robbing Aseneth of her birthright. From these authors, various new suggestions have been made, including 'The Conversion and Marriage of Aseneth' (Ross S. Kraemer, 'Women's Authorship of Jewish and Christian Literature in the Greco-Roman Period', in Levine, *'Women Like This'*, pp. 221-42 [222]).

A few observations are in order. Although Aseneth is in fact the single most important (human) character in the book, she is a figure whose significance emerges through her relation with others, most particularly through her relationship with Joseph in the first tale, and with the patriarchs as a group in the second. Although much of the first tale, including the poetic epilogue to the long version, is related from Aseneth's own perspective, the story actually militates against placing Aseneth in centre stage. After all, her autonomy and arrogance are seen as conditions to be overcome, as she submits to the Almighty, is joined to Israel, married to Joseph and rendered the mother of those seeking refuge. This dynamic is particularly emphasized in the longer recension, where the psalmic epilogue to the first tale (21.11-21) artfully directs the reader to see Aseneth's sin as not simple idolatry, but also an independent and scornful attitude. (See the diagrams on pages 41 and 43 of Humphrey, *The Ladies*, which disclose the chiastic sequence of this closing psalm, and its structural emphasis upon Aseneth's self-absorption). Aseneth has been wholly changed, not simply transferred her allegiance *pro forma* from idols to the true God. It needs to be emphasized that in the longer text Aseneth's hatred of *men* (Greek *andres*) is rather complex. In one sense, it is a virtue that safeguards her virginity, and which links her with Joseph, who hates all 'strange women'. As the story progresses, however, it is conceived as symptomatic of her overall arrogance with every human (Greek *anthrōpoi*); this relationship is seen both in the psalm, as reconstructed by

Burchard (21.17) and in the first description of Aseneth's character (2.1). According to the psalm, her self-absorbed and static condition—'*until* Joseph the Powerful One of God came' (v. 21)—is broken by the arrival of Joseph. (This is, in fact, borne out by the narrative, for Aseneth's aloof and disobedient demeanour changes instantly upon her sight of Joseph, a perception that seems far deeper than mere love-sickness.) The psalm goes on to celebrate Joseph *as God's agent*: first, he humbles her, then attracts her through beauty, wisdom and his spirit, and finally confirms and exalts her to a new status in the house of the Most High.

By virtue of its position, the psalmic epilogue has the final interpreting word and provides an exegesis of the first tale in terms of what *has happened* to Aseneth, not in terms of what she herself has done. The primary actor becomes not Aseneth, nor simply Joseph, but God, who has sent him (and his messenger double) to transform the heroine. In the second tale, we may perhaps expect to behold Aseneth's coming of age, and indeed find this maturity as she is encouraged to walk out alone without Joseph, 'because the Lord...himself will guard [her]' (26.2). However, even at this point she does not become the absolute centre of the story, although the plot rages around her attempted abduction and rescue. The virtuous quest to revenge her honour, a position articulated by the 'good' brothers, is relativized by the greater virtues of clemency, dependence upon God's justice and forgiveness:

> And Simeon said to her, 'Why does our mistress speak good (things) on behalf of her enemies? No, but let us cut them down with our swords, because they (were) first (to) plan evil (things) against us and against our father Israel and against our brother Joseph, this already twice, and against you, our mistress and queen, today.' And Aseneth stretched out her right hand...and said, 'By no means, brother, will you do evil for evil to your neighbor. To the Lord will you give (the right) to punish the insult (done) by them... [G]rant them pardon' (28.14).

Again, true heroism is understood as dependence upon the offstage divine Actor, 'seen' by Aseneth, Jacob, Joseph and Levi but evident in the story only through an unexpected sign.

It is not merely anachronistic, but also contrary to *Aseneth*'s clearly articulated world-view, to search for an autonomous heroine, or even a heroine of the Judith sort. Aseneth's 'passivity' is not simply an ideal for the feminine in an ancient patriarchal story, but becomes a model for all who 'worship God'. While the romantic genre is hospitable to the likes of Benjamin, whose strength is 'like a lion cub' (27.2) and to the sons of Leah who pursue their enemy with a speed 'like three-year old stags' (28.9), the peaceful confidence of Aseneth points away from this garden variety heroism. Her stance is in the end confirmed by Levi, the wise seer who tends their fallen foe, and returns him to his father Pharaoh, so that 'he will be our friend after this' (cf. Gen. 45.5, Joseph's own forgiveness of his brothers, and *The Letter of Aristeas* 227). Today's reader may be disappointed that Aseneth makes no further appearance after the high point of the story; probably the author and his earlier readers were unconcerned about this omission. (Interestingly, the modern Greek manuscript 671—tentatively dated in the seventeenth century—completes the tale by reference to the 'all-beautiful' Aseneth, and others go on to add a note about her sons.) The apocryphon is not, in the end, 'about' Aseneth alone, nor (obviously) about the late twentieth-century ideal of empowerment. Rather, we can deduce how the story was understood and received by many through the quaint subtitle attached to one manuscript: 'The wholesome Narrative concerning the corn-giving of Joseph, the all-fair, and concerning Aseneth, and how God united them' (noted in the introduction to Brooks's translation, p. 466). This tag, with its ethical and community-oriented accent, is a window into the world-view of the past, but not necessarily the earliest past of *Aseneth*'s author(s). *Aseneth* itself, while concerned for the 'wholesome', is far more rounded. The novel spins a story of intrigue, humanity and mysticism, and so celebrates the power of God to transform, bring to maturity and protect whoever (male or female) seeks refuge in the Most High. This is a tale not simply about Aseneth, nor about Joseph and Aseneth, but about a world in which God's revelations impinge upon the romantic and the everyday.

Versions of Aseneth and Patriarchalism

Recent students have been for the most part sensitive to these inner concerns of the novel. Yet there is also the question of the response of today's reader, and the ongoing search to reread texts so that they speak to today's questions. An interesting observation has been made by several scholars who contrast the two major text-types, and note that the shorter version seems more congenial to a feminist perspective. Often, this observation is joined to a judgment that the shorter version antedates the longer text; perhaps there is a suggestion of declension from a loftier ideal? At any rate, the peculiar quality of the short version is noted in various features, including, *sometimes*, a more prominent position of the character Aseneth in *Aseneth* (*P*). In the short version, for example, Aseneth is first introduced to the reader in wholly superlative terms, with reference to her arrogance and boastfulness omitted at 2.1*P*. Later, in

Joseph's prayer over her head, the adding of Aseneth to God's people is not detailed, with the result that the female protagonist Aseneth (rather than the community in general) is described as 'chosen' from beforetime:

Aseneth 8.9 (Burchard's text)	*Aseneth 8.10-11 (P)*
Lord God of my father Israel, the Most High,	O Lord, the God of my father Israel,
the Powerful One *of Jacob*,	the Most High, the Mighty One,
who gave life to all things…	Who didst quicken all things…
you, Lord, bless this virgin,	Do thou, O Lord…bless this virgin
and renew her by your spirit…	and renew her by thy spirit…
and let her eat your bread of life,	and may she eat the bread of thy life,
and drink your cup of blessing,	and may she drink the cup of thy
and number her among your people	blessing
that you have chosen before all came into	*She whom thou didst choose* before she
being,	was begotten
and let her enter your rest	And may she enter into thy rest
which you have prepared for your chosen	which thou has prepared for thine
ones,	elect.
and live in your eternal life for ever and ever.	
[italics mark key differences]	*[italics mark key differences]*

It is not that the shorter version actually changes any details about the heroine, for in both texts we hear later about Aseneth's name being written in God's book (15.4, but with less detail 15.3*P*). However, Joseph's prayer in the shorter version effectively exalts Aseneth at this very early point of the narrative, focusing attention on her chosenness, even before the reader hears her confessional prayer.

Again, in the shorter version's revelatory section, certain passages are not presented, with the result that Aseneth herself, and her heavenly archetype Metanoia take on much greater prominence. A comparison of the episode's structure in the two versions is intriguing:

Structure of Apocalypse (Burchard's text)

A Theophany **Who are you?** ch. 14
B Declaration **Who she will be** 15.1-10
C **Mystery** of name undivulged 15.11-12
B′ Verification by signs **Who she will be** 15.13-17.2
A′ Conclusion **I did not know [a] god** 17.3-10.

Structure of Apocalypse (P)

A Theophany **Who are you?** ch. 14
B Declaration **Who she will be and who Metanoia is** 15.1-8
C Verification by signs 15.9-17.2

D Conclusion **Be merciful…because I spoke evil in ignorance** 17.3-7.

In all, the longer version is more carefully structured, and also more complex, so that the reader is compelled to move in two directions—to recognize first the mysterious blessedness of the heavenly representatives; to recognize also the blessing that Aseneth receives, as a new inhabitant of that world. Section A's question about the Visitor's identity gives way to Section B's question of Aseneth's new status. The initial question is reintroduced but squashed by the Visitor in the central section C. We then return to the issue of Aseneth's identity in B', as the Visitor pronounces upon Aseneth' spiritual vision, confirms Joseph's earlier prayer that she eat, drink and be anointed as those in God's company, and reiterates her new status as a 'walled mother city of all who take refuge.' Finally, the concluding section A' returns to the initial question and the central mystery, as the Visitor and his chariot disappear in glory: Aseneth declares, 'I did not know that (a) god came to me.' The ambiguity of her statement may well be deliberate, since all through the epiphany there has been a conflation of the divine messenger with God (cf. the similar conflation in the Pentateuch's Angel of the Lord, e.g. Gen. 16.7, 13) as the Visitor speaks for God in the first person, shares his sublime and ineffable nature, and shines with his glory. The chiasm of the longer version, in fact, shelters section C, in which the unutterable quality of the heavenly Visitor is stressed.

All these details are missing in the shorter version, which does not evince a clear chiastic structure in its briefer narration. Just as the shorter version does not dwell upon the mystic receptivity of the female visionary, nor upon the esoteric description of the heavenly messenger in the epiphany and conclusion, so too it does not embed an unrevealed 'revelation' in the heart of the episode. Rather, the sequence of the short version moves in a more matter-of-fact fashion from start to finish, introducing first the divine agent, then his word about Aseneth's acceptance and her heavenly counterpart Metanoia, then some signs by which she is to know he is speaking truth, and then finally his departure, all responded to by a dutiful and humble penitent: 'Be merciful to me…' This disposition of material contrasts strongly with the chiastic longer version, so that the reader does not dwell upon the mysterious, but is thrust through the narrative quickly. In the short text, the major purpose of the revelation is to disclose details about Aseneth's new status and her connection with the heavenly realm, including some key ideas about her heavenly archetype Metanoia who intercedes for all who repent. The revelations, however, are brief, and impel the reader towards the ensuing narrative.

Metanoia's description (15.7-8 and 15.7-8*P*) in both versions is reminiscent of biblical and deutero-canonical descriptions of another feminine figure, Wisdom (Prov. 8; Sir. 4; Wis. 7–10). However, missing from the shorter version is the sibling link of Metanoia with the unnamed Visitor (which parallels the liaison of Joseph and Aseneth emphasized by Pentephres at 7.7 and Joseph himself at 7.8). Instead, she is highlighted as 'mother' of virgins (versus 'overseer' in the longer text), and the 'preparer of a heavenly bridal chamber [versus 'a place of rest'] *for those who love her*'. In the longer version, her characteristics as one who is 'pure', 'always laughing', 'gentle and meek' (compare 'pure' 'holy' and 'meek' in *P*) are explicitly appreciated by the Most High and the heavenly host. Kraemer sees these differences in Metanoia's description—her sibling relationship, her appreciation for these qualities—as indicative of 'a diminished portrait' (Kraemer, 'The Book of Aseneth', in *Searching the Scriptures*, p. 879) or 'domestication' in the longer version—either intentional, or the accidental result of added traditional details. In fact, it is a moot point whether the link to Joseph's heavenly double in the longer version is any more confining (from a contemporary feminist perspective) than Metanoia's description as a 'mother' rather than 'overseer': both versions define her in relational categories at one point or another. Moreover, her description in the longer version is arguably more active than that of the shorter version: 'gentleness' or 'forbearance' (*epieikēs*) is a characteristic traditionally ascribed to the Almighty (cf. Wis. 12.18; Bar. 2.27; *Aseneth* 11.10). We have already heard our penitent speak in her heart about the character of the Hebrew God, who has a gentleness that presupposes strength; here the quality is attributed also to his daughter Metanoia. In the same way, the rejoicing quality of the laughing Metanoia links her in the longer version more firmly with Wisdom, the companion of God (Prov. 8.30) Finally, 'meekness' is a quality associated not simply with the virtuous female, but with Joseph, as well (*Aseneth* 8.8). It is not, as Kraemer suggests, that Metanoia is appreciated for 'feminine' qualities in the long text, but that she mirrors the Almighty, and so patterns a stance to be embraced by all who join themselves to God in her name.

Far more interesting is the contrasting direction of 'love' in the two versions: in the shorter version, the onus is upon the penitent to 'love' Metanoia (15.11*P*), who will then reward them. In the longer text, stress is placed upon those who repent as 'beloved'—by Metanoia (15.7), and by God's unnamed messenger (15.8). (The emphasis on God's love is also consonant with the longer text's emphasis upon 'trusting in the Lord

God' in 15.7, which is omitted in the parallel 15.6*P*). Both themes, love for the divine and divine love, are in fact to be found in conjunction with Wisdom (cf. Prov. 8.17). By its omissions, however, the shorter version takes on a more moralistic and didactic character. It may be that Brooks in his English translation has captured something of the spirit of the short text by rendering *Metanoia* as 'Penitence'—a word that suggests an ongoing stance of returning to God. Interestingly, the shorter version also makes Aseneth's salvation of her repentant brothers-in-law more explicit, showing how Aseneth (human counterpart to Metanoia) becomes the figure of refuge for all who are penitent, and not simply for first-time converts. Is it possible that this emphasis points to the piety of a community in which ongoing repentance was stressed?—this theme, accompanied also by an archetypal angel, is prominent in the second-century *Shepherd of Hermas*.

In some respects, then, Aseneth appears to be placed more firmly at centre stage in the shorter version, along with her feminine angelic counterpart. However, missing from the short text (but present in longer) are several elements which round out the character of Aseneth in other ways—a deeper inner character revealed by her twice aborted confession (ch. 11), constant reference to her spiritual sight, her use of wisdom language, and mystical descriptions of her physical presence. In the short version, for example, we do not hear that she has 'fine hands like a scribe' (20.5), nor is her transfiguration highlighted and noted by every key character, as it is in the longer version. Again, the blessing of her seven virginal companions is not accompanied by a reference to the 'seven pillars' of Wisdom (17.6 *versus* 17.5*P*), and so Aseneth loses an explicit link with a famous Hebrew Bible image.

Some have concentrated upon the more distinct biblical echoes of the longer version, and argued that this is elaborative. Others have read the extended passages in the longer text as presenting a less independent Aseneth, more in need of masculine command, motivation and approval. Angela Standhartinger is most insistent in this regard, arguing that the two versions are 'not incidental products' but that they each present a different 'image of women' ('From Fictional Text to Socio-Historical Context', in *SBLSP 1996* [Atlanta, GA: Scholars Press, 1996], pp. 302-18 [305]). Thus, she cites, in the longer version, Aseneth's lowered eyes before God's messenger, the continued emphasis on her fear throughout the revelatory section, and the building of a honeycomb upon her mouth as an obstacle to speech. Careful analysis is demanded at these points.

First, although 14.9 and 14.8*P*) differ in wording, so that only the
shorter version has Aseneth raise her *eyes* ('head' in the longer version),
in a previous episode (11.19//12.1*P*), it is the *longer* version that is
more pointed about an open-faced and verbal Aseneth. Again, the continued fear of Aseneth is not to be construed as a feminine reaction, but
as the stance of a seer who rightly perceives the transcendent: in 16.12-
14, Aseneth's understanding of the comb's origin is received apprecia-
tively, not (*pace* Standhartinger) patronizingly, by the Visitor, who in
the longer text blesses her by grasping her head with his glorious hand
and then gives a verbal benediction concerning her wisdom and new
status. Given this emphasis, it is hard to follow Standhartinger's reasoning that the honeycomb built on Aseneth's lips must render her mute!
Surely, as the comb is related to Torah and Wisdom (through the
ongoing tradition of Ps. 19/18 LXX through to Sir. 24), this strange
vision is symbolic of her understanding and ability to speak wisely. The
comb comes from the messenger's mouth and is now associated with
the mouth of Aseneth. Similarly, Standhartinger makes much of the
'boldness' of which Aseneth repents after the Visitor has left (17.9) and
contrasts this with the 'boldness' of Levi, which is later applauded at
23.10: her conclusion is that this quality is applauded in males, but to
be avoided in the pious woman. In fact, Aseneth's repentance of her
boldness does not spring from an appreciation of gender-specified roles,
but reflects upon her previous ignorance: 'Be gracious, Lord…because
I have spoken boldly before you all my words in ignorance' (17.10).
The fear of the Lord as the beginning of wisdom is not a gender-
specific precept.

Similarly questionable is Standhartinger's understanding of Aseneth's
transformed appearance in the longer text (18.9-10). She sees this as cul-
turally conditioned according to gender, since only the bust of the heroine, minus any active limb, is detailed. (This static description is avoided
in the short text, which only pictures her shining face and eyes at 18.7*P*).
The longer text, however, supposedly presents Aseneth through 'the
ancients' optics of beauty' ('From Fictional Context', p. 313) and is to be
contrasted with the fuller presentation of a male figure Jacob, with arms,
sinews, thighs and feet, in ch. 22. Several comments are to be made.
First, Aseneth is viewing herself in a basin, and so in the terms of the
story would not see her full figure Second, the description of her
reflection in terms of prosperous fighting men, and red 'like a son of
man's' blood, is hardly passive. This is particularly striking when we
compare Aseneth's description against the diminutive and sentimental

imagery of more purely erotic passages, either Jewish (e.g. Song 4) or Hellenistic (Standhartinger cites the first-century poet Rufinus, translated by Paton in *Anthologia Graeca* 5.48). Although the features described—cheeks, lips, teeth, hair, neck, breasts—fit with the erotic genre, the manner of description is more reminiscent of strong and fruitful Wisdom in Sir. 24.13-17, a passage that also informs the earlier angelic blessing at *Aseneth* 16.16. The differences in the texts again seem due more to a calculated use of traditional materials in the longer text than to a particular view of women. It is also significant that those who behold Aseneth's new form (mostly males) are filled with fear and amazed (18.11; 19.5; 20.7; 21.3), just as Aseneth had responded to the heavenly Visitor—for 'her beauty was like heavenly beauty' (20.6).

So far the arguments concerning a more patriarchal character of the longer text seems like special pleading. Ross Kraemer, who comes to many of the same conclusions as Standhartinger, but who pursues a more nuanced method, does point out an important difference between the texts at 8.5 (cf. 8.4P). The phrase 'and her breasts were already standing up like handsome apples' is seemingly an erotic detail that finds no place in the short text. It may be that the imagery serves more than an erotic aim at this point (on this see my reading in Chapter 3). If some ancient sensibilities read this explicit language as 'denigrating' (Kraemer, 'Women's Authorship,' p. 234) to the character of Aseneth, then its omission (or addition) may be telling. However, attention to the manuscripts themselves shows that this phrase is found neither in *d* (Philonenko's preferred family) nor in *b* (Burchard's base text) but in family *a* (Burchard, *OTP*, II, p. 211 n. h), which is agreed by all to be a later elaborating text. Burchard's decision to include the phrase reflects his judgment on this passage, and need not be considered definitive in a comparison of the text-types. That is, the phrase may be a romanticizing addition, and not reflective of the view of women in either contestant for the earliest text.

Cited also in favour of a female-oriented shorter text is its supposedly less-pronounced father imagery. Naturally, there is less reference to God as father in the shorter text, since the locale for these—the two preparatory silent speeches of Aseneth in the confession sequence—is omitted. In the confession itself, the extended simile of 12.7P, where Aseneth appeals to God 'as to a father *and mother*', is intriguing, particularly since this version tends towards concision but atypically includes an extended image at this point. Nevertheless, this brief note is hardly sufficient to indicate a different theology, particularly as the shorter text also goes on to speak only of God as a father, and does not pursue the feminine metaphor. The absence of the note about Aseneth's breasts, and the appeal to father and mother, when compounded with other structural features (e.g. the solo appearance of Repentance in ch. 15, the chosenness of Aseneth before her birth, and fewer mediating scenes between Aseneth and others) may render the shorter text more congenial to today's reader. However, the assessment of these details is complex, as we have seen. A reaction in favour of the short text may be more indicative of our tastes than a careful reflection of this text's own voice. I suspect that ancient readers of *d* family, could they be engaged in conversation, would be astonished at the conclusions drawn today about the *Aseneth* that they knew. Further, the structural de-centring of *Aseneth* in the *b* text makes for a narrative intent on mystery and the exaltation of the divine, not on the subordination of women. Neither text can be easily coopted, positively or negatively, for feminist concerns.

Aseneth's Satus and Social Realities
This analysis of feminist readings and comparisons of versions has demonstrated yet again the perils of quick assumptions in the reading of ancient texts. Decisions made about *Aseneth* are particularly complex in that we are considering versions of various lengths and shapes, with intricate relationships to traditional texts. Equally difficult is the use of this unusual double novella to illuminate our understanding of social realities in the ancient world—the romance may describe desired rather than actual circumstances, its characters may take on symbolic proportions rather than imitate actual persons, and so on. May we even agree with one critic that 'the focus [of *Aseneth*]...is on women' (Mary R. Lefkowitz, 'Did Ancient Women Write Novels?', in Levine [ed.], *'Women Like This'*, pp. 199-219 [219]). As Kraemer notes, in our text 'the portraits of both women and men are highly artificial' ('The Book of Aseneth', p. 885). Given Aseneth's archetypal function in the novel, it is hasty even to assume that those characteristics, blessings and actions associated with the heroine are reflective of realities or aspirations for *women* in particular.

With these cautions in mind, several tentative observations may be made. The first is that *Aseneth* does not assume a polemical air in its ascription of spiritual qualities to a *woman*—what keeps Aseneth from the blessing foreshadowed by Joseph is not her femaleness but her idolatry, a quality associated with arrogance and self-reliance. That Pharaoh's son is also infected with this disease, and that Joseph and Levi also display meekness, is confirmation that the ideal is not conceived according to gender. Alongside the ideal of human meekness, the novel assumes that it is appropriate for women (particularly august women of patriarchal times) to take on prophetic or visionary functions; it does not, in any overt way, argue for this as a freedom to be pursued. Aseneth's transformed character is held up as a pattern to all—male or female—who would seek refuge with the Most High, but it is not clear that those emulating her should seek or expect similar mystical vision and perception.

It is in the domestic scenes between Aseneth and her family that we may see some indication of female experience in antiquity, though even here caution is in order. It may be that the archaising flavour of the piece, purportedly set in Joseph's Egypt, obscures our insight into the relationship between the sexes, or what was considered to be the appropriate domains of unmarried and married women, at the time of the author/original readers. We may, for example, be tempted to read Aseneth's initial seclusion as a well-accepted ideal, and point to the 'inside' space allotted to unmarried women in antiquity. In this case, Aseneth's relative freedom in the second tale may indicate a distinction between virginal seclusion and married liberty. In both cases, however, there is reason to question whether the story is to be read 'straight'. Aseneth's purity, for example, is exaggerated to the point of absurdity in the initial sequences, as we are told repeatedly of the purity of her chamber, of her bed, of the virgins who keep company with her, of the distance from even male children, and so on. References to the high tower, to the three chambers and windows, and to the seven companions reinforce the impression that this enclosure is traditional, perhaps fictional and romantic: 'a garden enclosed is my sister, my bride' (Song of Solomon 4.12). Similarly, the unusual character of Aseneth's *sortie* without her husband in ch. 26 is both stressed by Aseneth's premonitory fears and answered by her husband's reference to divine protection. It is unlikely that the author intends his reader to envision or even to idealize married women gallivanting around the countryside, and so exposing themselves to danger—Aseneth's escapade is altogether exceptional, and her freedom designed to precipitate an adventure that features a divine rescue. No doubt the reader is intended to imitate Aseneth's attitude—her confidence in God, as well as her forgiving clemency; whether she is being invited actually to enact the freedom of this high-born and divinely chosen ancient 'lady' is unclear. The difficulty here is in determining the difference between archetypal symbol and role model—a distinction not always made by critics. (See, for example, Pervo, 'Aseneth and her Sisters', p. 154.)

The literary signals, then, suggest that in this fictive, far-away world, virgins were totally secluded and married, godly women might well tempt fate by their liberties. It is unlikely, however, that either extreme represents the social dynamics of the author's time. More promising is the relationship between Aseneth and her parents, although the dialogue between them may also assume an archaic air for the purposes of the romance. Is the silence of Aseneth's mother a remnant of cultural verisimilitude (i.e. reflective of the author's time) or a feature of the story's setting in Genesis? Again, it is hard to say whether a daughter in the author's circle would address her father in the formal third person, as does Aseneth, or whether this is novelistic dialogue. We can see that her form of address does not represent a consistent textual tradition, since there are variations in both the *b* family and in early translations. Those who compare Burchard's text with Philonenko's will see slight differences here, but the variation between all texts is even greater, suggesting that various redactors and translators adapted this particular scene to suit their reader's sensibilities.

The general playing out of Aseneth's refusal to marry Joseph reads naturally within the story, and probably indicates ancient standards related to honour and shame, standards that would be shared by the author(s) and readers. Aseneth's class consciousness is not repudiated by her father, who in fact has introduced Joseph as a desirable suitor because of his status. Her boldness against her father is apparent enough, but not overstressed, either. There is no direct narratival moralizing against filial impiety, but the narrator merely implies this by commenting on Pentephres's reaction to his daughter's outburst. Here again, the number of variant readings discloses the discomfort of various readerships with a potentially explosive interaction between daughter and her father. Some witnesses present a more saccharine and/or more daring Aseneth: 'No, my lord father and my sweetest mother'; 'No, my father, not to this one will I be joined'; 'Anyway, O my precious father, be silent and do not speak to me such words.' (See the variants given in Burchard's footnotes, p. 207.) Here again we note differences in the dynamics between fathers and wayward daughters by comparing the texts of Philonenko and Burchard: 'Pentephres was ashamed to speak further to his daughter' (4.12) seems to have been amended to 'Pentephres thought it wiser to say no more…' (4.16P). It is possible that the author of the shorter version was less shocked by the adolescent's behaviour, and simply ascribes a psychological wisdom to Pentephres. Thus, the issues of honour and shame are displaced by parental tactics of dealing with a headstrong girl. This change in nuance coheres with the shorter text's lack of emphasis upon Aseneth's pride. Whether or not such changes point to a change in societal dynamics is a question worth asking, but difficult to answer. At any rate, in both versions the story goes on to confirm a father's choice: what Pentephres cannot engineer, God himself will manage, through the arresting meeting of the god-like Joseph with Aseneth herself. In the end, neither text applauds autonomy: the shorter text simply does not stress Aseneth's character flaws, thus creating an exemplary heroine for its drama.

Female Authorship?

Aseneth is unusual in that it highlights a woman's story, complete with inner turmoil and revelatory experience; this feature has led some to speculate about the gender of the author. Answers to this question have been varied: *Aseneth* may well have been written by a woman, especially in its shorter version, which presents a more independent view of women (Angela Standhartinger, *Das Frauenbild im Judentum der hellenistischen Zeit: Ein Beitrag anhand von 'Joseph und Aseneth'* [*AGJU* 26; Leiden: E.J. Brill, 1995], pp. 225-37); *Aseneth* could never have been written by a woman, because it is hopelessly patriarchal (Lefkowitz). Those who highlight the 'feminist' tendencies of the romance, or versions of it, have tended to entertain the possibility of female authorship; those who have been offended by its pervasive hierarchical view have denied this. Some, such as Ross Kraemer, have been wise enough to realize that even a patriarchally conceived narrative could have been written by a woman, since this world-view was general in the ancient world, and not limited to the male imagination.

Other indices of female authorship have been found in the *realia* drawn from the sphere of women—for example, interest in food, apparel, interior design or female companions. The presence of these in *Aseneth* has been weighed differently by different authors, since some see in-depth description of such details as serving symbolic aims rather than indicating female experience. In particular, descriptions of Aseneth, of the bees' clothing or of her chambers have been featured in symbolic readings of the text. Again, some have viewed Aseneth's tenderness for her female companions as a sign of female authorship, while others have suggested the symbolic importance of these virgins for the text. All these features—domestic familiarity and mysticism—rendered the novel of interest to women in the ancient world. Such details are not clearly indicative of female authorship, nor is the characterization a clear pointer to the female perspective, however. Some (e.g. Standhartinger, 'From Fictional', p. 317) have noted the irony with which the male protagonists are treated in the book. Pharaoh, a male, is presented as the one who is love-crazed, in contrast to the more common trope of a woman thus afflicted; Aseneth's cry for help evokes an act of God whereby the male weapons of swords are cast down and supernaturally dissolve. Unfortunately, the irony in both cases is more likely directed against autonomous pride, and not against machismo, since Aseneth herself comes in for both subtle and direct chastisement on the same score.

In the end, we are left with inconclusive evidence regarding authorship and gender. Ross Kraemer, who once considered *Aseneth* a likely candidate for female authorship, has now adopted a more agnostic stance (*When Aseneth*, p. 215). This change in opinion is a salutary model, reminding the reader to avoid an anachronistic imposition of values upon an ancient text. Particularly problematic will be those studies which attempt to draw trajectories from one textual tradition to another, on the sole basis of observations having to do with gender construal and gender relations. Any such reconstruction will need to proceed with great caution, recognizing that trends in societies do not move with predictability or smoothness, and in full acknowldgement that the genre of *Aseneth* obscures the social realities of its own author(s) and ancient readers.

Further Reading

Burchard, C., 'Joseph and Aseneth', in J.H. Charlesworth (ed.), *The Old Testament Pseudepigrapha*, II (2 vols.; Garden City, NY: Doubleday, 1983-85), pp. 177-247.

Chesnutt, Randall D., 'Revelatory Experiences Attributed to Biblical Women', in Amy-Jill Levine (ed.), *'Women Like This': New Perspectives on Jewish Women in the Greco-Roman World* (Atlanta: Scholars Press, 1991), pp. 107-25. A nuanced discussion of this issue.

Doty, Susan Elizabeth Hog, 'From Ivory Tower to City of Refuge: The Role and Function of the Protagonist in "Joseph and Aseneth" and Related Narratives' (unpublished dissertation, Iliff School of Theology and University of Denver, 1989). Feminist analysis of *Aseneth* in relation to other novels, limited by Philonenko's text.

Humphrey, E.M., *The Ladies and the Cities: Transformations and Apocalyptic Identity in Joseph and Aseneth, 4 Ezra, The Apocalypse and The Shepherd of Hermas* (JSPSup, 17; Sheffield: Sheffield Academic Press, 1995).

Lefkowitz, Mary R., 'Did Ancient Women Write Novels?', in Levine (ed.), *'Women Like This'*, pp. 199-219. Interesting comparison of several apocryphal writings, marred by anachronistic thinking.

Paxson, James J., 'Personification's Gender', *Rhetorica* 16 (1998), pp. 149-79. An intriguing interdisciplinary study of metaphor and gender, with obviously applicability to *Aseneth*.

Pervo, Richard I., 'Aseneth and Her Sisters: Women in Jewish Narrative and in the Greek Novels', in Levine (ed.), *'Women Like This'*, pp. 145-60. Pervo is typically masterful on genre, but perhaps too eager to find feminist models in ancient literature.

Kraemer, Ross S., 'The Book of Aseneth', in E. Schüssler Fiorenza (ed.), *Searching the Scriptures: A Feminist Commentary*, II (Atlanta, GA: Scholars Press, 1994), pp. 787-816.

—'Women's Authorship of Jewish and Christian Literature in the Greco-Roman Period', in Levine (ed.), *'Women Like This'*, pp. 221-42. See also Chapter 7 of *When Aseneth Met Joseph: A Late Antique Tale of the Biblical Patriarch and his Egyptian Wife, Reconsidered* (New York: Oxford University Press, 1998).

Standhartinger, Angela, *Das Frauenbild im Judentum der hellenistischen Zeit: Ein Beitrag anhand von 'Joseph und Aseneth'* (AGJU 26; Leiden: E.J. Brill, 1995). Argues for a distinct view of women in the longer and shorter texts. See also 'From Fictional Text to Socio-Historical Context', in *SBLSP 1996* (Atlanta: Scholars Press, 1996), pp. 302-18.

3

A RHETORICAL-LITERARY READING OF *ASENETH*

An introduction to the issues concerning *Aseneth* that have plagued scholars is helpful as an orientation not only to this particular apocryphon but also to the questions that can and must be asked about any fictional ancient work. The approaches and methods used for such investigations, however, often do not promote an appreciation of the writing itself: they seek to read between, behind or even (in a 'hermeneutic of suspicion') *against* the lines, rather than concentrating upon the narrative. While an awareness of the many issues surrounding *Aseneth* is essential if the student is to read intelligently, the very nature of this piece encourages us to move on to a 'second naïveté'. It would seem that there is in *Aseneth* something akin to the dynamics of S. Morgenstern's *Princess Bride*, that is, an appeal to readers of different levels, without the loss of its primary characteristic as a *persuasive story*. In speaking of *story*, we need to pay attention to the *what* of the work—time and action (or stasis, the cessation of these), characters, tone and speech, recurring or transformed motifs and images, plot and structure. In speaking of *persuasion*, we will consider these same elements in terms of *Aseneth*'s *why* and *how*—what reasons can we find for the work's features, and how did they and do they affect the reader(s)?

When one considers a biblical narrative, its rhetorical dimension is evident: this work has found its way into a privileged place within a religious community not simply because of its aesthetic value, which may or may not be superlative. Presumably, the work is there (among other reasons) because a community has recognized its power to encourage, edify or transform according to the character of the faith of which it is partially constitutive. Although aesthetic analysis (i.e. literary analysis) will often also be appropriate, rhetorical analysis of the work is therefore demanded by the very nature of biblical material. (One thinks immediately of the penultimate epilogue to the fourth gospel: 'These things are written *that you* may believe,' Jn 20.31). This call for rhetorical study is not so immediately apparent with a work like *Aseneth*, which might be dismissed as yet another example of a beguiling tale. (Indeed, those who despise popular works might consider literary analysis too high-flown for *Aseneth*, although the work, as a narrative, begs for such a treatment!) However, the parabiblical nature of the work, its paraenetic character, and its preservation (sometimes even in conjunction with the canon) by various communities, suggest that *Aseneth* needs to be understood in terms of rhetoric.

Such an analysis calls for a different method than is often adopted by those who isolate and analyse literary 'speeches' within larger complexes and then compare them to the classical models. That procedure, while fruitful, is insufficient to demonstrate the overall rhetorical impact of a narrative. Rather, a delicate balance of rhetorical and literary analysis is indicated in a work of this sort. Indeed, *Aseneth* shares its curious characteristics with other narratives (some canonical) that link vision with argument, bringing together evocative imagery and directive polemic in various ways. Frequently, vision-reports are embedded within larger host genres. This is certainly the case with *Aseneth*, where the epiphany and revelations of the Visitor are crucial to the development of the plot. Preliminary study of other such narratives suggests several different possible combinations of story, vision and argumentation. (See studies of Humphrey and the volume edited by Bloomquist and Carey in 'Further Reading' pp. 111-13). Sometimes vision-reports emerge as carefully crafted pieces that form an integral part of the persuasive line. One thinks immediately of Luke's use of vision to introduce key themes, or of Paul's reluctant revelation in 2 Corinthians 12, which brings a classic fool's speech to a stunning climax. Other vision-reports are less central to the host genre, yet still make an interesting contribution to the rhetorical effect of each passage. Sometimes a vision will complicate the rhetorical direction of the discourse or narrative, or even abandon the major thrust of the story, because of the centrifugal and evocative character of its visionary symbols and images.

In the reading of *Aseneth*, it will be important to treat the work as a narrative that creates its own world, and yet which directs the reader according to a certain purpose (or several purposes). It will also be necessary, considering the extensive nature of the vision sequence, to ask how this revelatory section is integrated with the story and with its perceived rhetoric. The quest is difficult, since discussion of rhetoric can

tend to rob a narrative (especially a vision!) of its living quality, reducing this to a proposition, teaching or statement of purpose. Fortunately,
the allusive quality of the story, which in this case is replete with enigmatic symbols and motifs, will work against such a reduction. Yet it is
clear that the reader must not abandon *Aseneth* to the world of sheer
aesthetics—here is a tantalizing story that pronounces its riddles and
asks to be understood, not merely enjoyed. We move on, then, to a lit-
erary-rhetorical reading of *Aseneth* that will attempt to do justice to its
unusual narrative and rhetoric. Because we are dealing with an entire
book, it is not possible to consider all literary and rhetorical aspects.
Rather, each of the major sections of *Aseneth* will be read separately in
terms of four general categories: time, space and action; characters and
imagery; discourse and tone; and plot and structure. Where it is
deemed helpful to the illumination of a specific passage, structural disposition and/or rhetorical flow will be diagrammed. Finally, in deference to the book's popular character, we will consider from time to
time the initial response of a biblically informed nine-year-old, who
heard *Aseneth* read aloud on a rainy summer afternoon. The overall
shape and rhetoric of the story will be seen as emerging from all these
features, particularly in the orchestration of discourse, and in what is
understated, emphasized or transformed.

1. 'Once Upon a Time' (Chapters 1–9)

Time, Space and Action

'And it happened'—a phrase that echoes the introductory words of
Joshua, Judges, Ruth, 2 Samuel and 1 Maccabees—is the reader's first
clue as to how *Aseneth* is to be read. Action will be important to this
piece, and it will be significant action, action like that found in the
books of old. As with the biblical books that use this phrase, the story is
situated in 'time', the specific time borrowed from the Genesis narrative, in which Joseph gathers grain during the years of plenty: it is harvest. The implications of the year, month and day remain elusive for
today's reader, and various suggestions (Burchard, *OTP*, II, p. 202)
have been made by reference to the calendar of another parabiblical
book, *Jubilees*. Is Joseph unconcerned about the Sabbath, as his departure date suggests, and is it significant that his 'epiphany' in the region
surrounding 'The City of the Sun' (*Heliopolis*) will take place on the
summer solstice? It is difficult to be sure, but the resonance of the harvest season—a contradiction, it would seem, to the solstice is cross-cul-

tural. No doubt, Joseph's most important 'gathering' will be the in-bringing of Aseneth. The appropriateness of this setting is confirmed by the contrasting famine setting of the second story (22.1) in which adversity must be overcome.

Time and action, then, attract the attention of the reader immediately, as does space. The narrator uses a 'zoom' technique, moving our attention from the 'whole land' of Egypt (1.1) into the 'territory of Heliopolis' (1.2), and finally into 'that city' (1.3)—the route travelled by Joseph. Aseneth, while not herself mobile, has a fame that has 'spread over all that land and to the ends of the inhabited world' (2.6). This outward movement follows immediately upon our tracing of Joseph's path into Heliopolis; it is accentuated by the description of outside affairs, as various nobles and princes fight over Aseneth, and as a betrothed Moabite princess is rejected by Pharaoh's son on Aseneth's account. Within this double pattern of movement (Joseph *in* to Heliopolis, Aseneth's fame *out* to the whole *oikumenē*), we are introduced to the key players: Joseph, the active one who is sent on a quest; Aseneth, the one around whom all the action spins. Connected to the key figures are Pharaoh, who acts as the ordainer of the action, Pentephres, the father who nurtures and protects the heroine, and Pharaoh's son, who will become the antagonist in the second narrative. From its inception, then, we encounter the themes of outside and inside, of kin and stranger, that will dominate the story. The 'softness' of the boundaries between these categories is also intimated, both in the introduction of the Gentile priest, who is 'exceedingly rich and prudent and gentle' (1.3) and in the initial description of Aseneth, who has 'nothing similar to…the Egyptians' but is 'in every respect similar to the daughters of the Hebrews' (1.5). Already in the first chapter, biblical connection has been established, action commenced, key figures described, motifs suggested and the plots of both narratives (1-21; 22-29) foreshadowed.

Chapter 2 extends and intensifies the sense of stasis that has followed immediately upon the introduction of Joseph's activity at 1.2. (The rehearsal of Joseph's actions will in fact not be resumed until 3.1.) The narrator continues to elaborate upon Pentephres's daughter, and the environs where 'her virginity was being fostered' (2.7). The seclusion of Aseneth is mirrored by the disposition of details: the tower and its height is described along with the glory of Aseneth's three rooms, then various antechambers (all seven of them!) to Aseneth's own room, and then that room itself, with its golden bed, on which 'Aseneth slept, *alone*; and a man or another woman never sat on it, only Aseneth, *alone*', then the court surrounding the house, then the wall around the court, then the four iron-plated gates guarded by 18 powerful young men. Again, the narrator moves his reader in two directions—*in* to the 'holy of holies' and back out to the battlements that protect this virginal place.

And so 'it happens' again (3.1): the narration resumes at the point where Joseph nears Heliopolis, pre-announced by 12 attendants. Again, the time is stressed, as is the hour of the day: full noon is an appropriate time for the 'Powerful One of God' to arrive, although we will not view his sun-like appearance for two more chapters. Again, action is suspended, so that the hero arrives in stages, first at the city limits (3.2), and then at the doors of the courtyard (5.1). Between these stages, we view a relatively static Aseneth, unaware of Joseph's impending visit, elaborately dressing. Yet much action continues within the household of Pentephres, who with his wife has just arrived from their estate in the country *for it was the time of harvest* (3.5 in the longer version). Pentephres sends off his steward in a hurry (3.4) to make preparations for Joseph, and joins Aseneth, who has been preparing herself hurriedly to meet her father and mother. She receives the produce of the field from them and then is invited to sit between them for a consultation on marriage, which is aborted both by her refusal and by the announced arrival of Joseph at the gate (5.1). Aseneth flees the scene, going upstairs to view the visitor in safety, while her parents ceremoniously greet the guest and bring him with care into their home. Action words stud the narrative: 'call', 'hurry', 'prepare', 'make ready', 'dressed', 'went down', 'came', 'sit down', 'grasp', 'poured', 'rushed in', 'fled', 'went up', 'went out', 'opened', 'entered', 'drew tight', 'closed', 'prostrated themselves', 'descended', 'greeted'. Aseneth's calm and secure world has been shattered by a flurry of excitement.

At 6.1, the action is further stilled, as the reader is admitted to the inner perspective of Aseneth: 'Aseneth…was strongly cut (to the heart), and her soul was crushed…and she was filled with great fear' (6.1). However, the burden of her soliloquy is not her own 'wretched' condition, but the 'sun from heaven' which has '*come*…on its chariot and *entered* our house today' (6.2). In this way, the emphasis is placed on Joseph as quester, a theme that is continued as Aseneth muses on her inability to hide from this one whose very gaze cannot be eluded, because 'nothing hidden escapes him' (6.6). Joseph's eyes are (in accord with ancient physiology) described as possessing active energy, illumined by an inner divine source of light. At Aseneth's time of stasis, the untir-

3. *A Rhetorical-Literary Reading of Aseneth*   85

ing and relentless quest of God's messenger is acknowledged—his search
will rescue our 'wretched' and 'ignorant' heroine. Though paralysed at
this point, Aseneth prays that the 'God of Joseph' will be gracious, so
that she may again be active, if only as a servant to Joseph (6.8).
Action resumes as Joseph enters, beyond the courtyard, into the very
house of Pentephres, and, sitting on the throne, eats at his specially
appointed table. As Aseneth feared, his eyes find her out (7.2), and he
recognizes (or perhaps mistakes) her for a 'strange woman'. Pentephres
commends his daughter as a chaste virgin, however, and Joseph gives
permission for her to 'come'. More activity: Aseneth's mother 'goes
up' (8.1) and brings Aseneth down before Joseph; she is obedient to
her father's command to greet Joseph. The compliment is returned, but
Joseph will not seal this with a kiss: Aseneth comes forward, but is
physically restrained by Joseph, who explains with very active language
(mouths blessing, eating, drinking, and anointing oneself) the difference
between Godfearers and idolaters. The very words are effective. For
the second time Aseneth is 'cut to the heart', and, gazing at Joseph
with tear-filled eyes, receives what he *can* give—not yet a kiss, but a
blessing accompanied by his right hand. Within this benediction, it is
God, the active creator and caller, who is asked to bless, renew, form
anew, make alive again, allow to eat and drink, and enumerate among
his people (whom he has chosen). Aseneth's reaction is ambivalent but
forceful: at first joyful, she hurries up to solitude but falls on her bed in
dismay and joy as a result of the word 'spoken to her in the name of
the Most High God' (9.1). With the greatest force possible, she repents
of idolatry, and then *waits*. Joseph resumes his immediate activity of
eating, and then goes on his customary active way in harnessed horses,
driving around the land, 'because this is the day on which God began
to make all his creatures'. He leaves with a promise to return and *lodge*
in this home 'on the eighth day' (9.5): it is just possible that this
unusual verb *aulizomai* plays upon the instruction in Sirach to 'lodge' in
wisdom's home (Sir. 51.23), for despite Aseneth's failures, her affinities
with Wisdom will increase as the narrative progresses. (On this
dynamic, see Kraemer, *When Aseneth*, pp. 22-27.)

Throughout this first part, then, we see the interplay between stasis
and movement, and note the great importance of space—near, far,
high, low. Although her life is one of stationary seclusion, the limited
actions of Aseneth are significant: in arrogance, Aseneth goes up, in
obedience she comes down, catalysed by the blessing; she goes up again
to do what she is able, and waits to see what will happen. Joseph is

marked, on the other hand, by activity, although the narrative insists throughout that the true initiator is God. This feature is emphasized by the fact that the father-figure, Pentephres, cannot accomplish his goal to join Aseneth with Joseph. We know already at the conclusion of ch. 9 that what cannot be done by humans, God will fulfil: God will 'bless this virgin', and has indeed begun this new work through the agency of the questing Joseph. An 'actantial' chart of the surface structure is helpful in seeing the complex relationship of the characters:

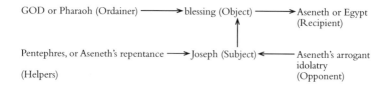

On the larger level of the story, that is, Joseph's quest for grain on Pharaoh's command, there is no opponent: readers of the biblical story know already of Joseph's great success. The placing of Aseneth into this context implies also that there is no real opposition to Joseph's greater task of blessing his 'intended': already on seeing him, her arrogance has crumbled; already on hearing his blessing, her idolatry has been eschewed. Just as Joseph is the unhampered gatherer of grain, so he will be successful in the matter of Aseneth. Let us turn now to consider the characters themselves, and the motifs by which they are described.

Characters and Imagery

Aseneth's beauty and her tower existence follow the conventions of other famous romances, such as the Demotic Egyptian story of Tabubu (also a priest's daughter), who lived high in a lofty house with a garden complex. Although it is difficult to be certain about tone, it appears that in the prolix description and insistent emphasis upon virginity, *Aseneth* exaggerates these conventions, assuming comic dimensions. Virginity is not simply the absence of sexual relations, but a state to be 'nurtured' (2.7); that Aseneth is already 18 suggests that the fostering has already gone on for some time. At every point, there are details that underscore her purity: one storeroom contains the ornaments of her virginity; seven others house virgins who have never even spoken with a male child; the climactic description of the innermost chamber stresses twice the 'aloneness' of the heroine. But there is a fly in the ointment! Aseneth's physical purity is not matched by her spiritual state, since she worships innumerable Egyptian gods and sacrifices to them every day (2.3). Our perceptive younger reader is slightly puzzled at this point: 'But that's *bad*, isn't it?' Obviously she had not been expecting a beautiful and virtuous heroine to be given a black mark against her character so early in the story, and had passed over Aseneth's 'boastful arrogance' (2.1) because of the uncouth clamouring of her many suitors.

This disjuncture in Aseneth's character is in fact underscored in several ways: by the arrangements of her chambers, and by her initial appearance before her parents. Although the narrative is not completely unambiguous, her bedroom seems to be the very room that is given over to worship, so that physical virginity and spiritual 'adultery' are juxtaposed—her inner chamber is a shrine to both states. In its positive aspect, the tower evokes several images for the knowing reader, including that of the house of Wisdom, and that of a temple: this prudent priest has a daughter who is accompanied by seven virgins, soon to become 'pillars' (cf. Prov. 9.1). The number seven may evoke ancient depictions of the heavens (Qumran's *Songs of the Sabbath Sacrifice*; *2 En.* 20.1 [short version]; *Asc. Isa.* 7.1), a concept that may also inform *Aseneth* 22.13, though the reading is uncertain. Again, Aseneth's three rooms recall temple architecture, while they also enshrine foreign food and idols. Aseneth's abode itself contains contradictory imagery, an indication of its inhabitant.

Similarly, as Aseneth comes to greet her parents, there is a juxtaposition of opposites. She dresses herself in white, violet and gold, and with ornaments of her virginity and her idolatry. Strange names and faces glitter from everywhere on her person, though she is dressed in bridal and noble attire. The veil itself is ambivalent symbol, suggesting either modesty or harlotry (cf. Song 1.7b; Gen. 38.14-15). Her attire, then, foreshadows what she will become ('a bride of God', 4.1) but also presents her as one who is ignorant of the God of Jacob. This ambiguity in Aseneth's character, suggested in the description of her abode and of her person, is also intimated by the dialogue in ch. 7 between Pentephres and Joseph, and the 'flashback' to conversation between Joseph and his own father, Jacob. Joseph's sight of Aseneth at the window creates a background debate: is she a 'strange woman' (Prov. 7.4) to be avoided by Joseph, or one like 'a sister' (cf. the picture of Wisdom in Prov. 7.5) to him? The rich content of Aseneth's chamber, her attire, even her repudiation of men, can all be read in opposing directions. Is her storeroom full of delicacies to seduce (*Aseneth* 7.4; cf. Prov. 7.16-17), or with riches to delight and nourish (Prov. 24.3-40). Is she dressed

as a seductress, as the virtuous woman (Prov. 31.22), or even as
Wisdom herself (Sir. 6.30-31). Is her virginity a symbol of purity or of
arrogance? In contrast, there is little ambiguity in the epiphanic description of
Joseph (5.4-5), although the author draws the imagery from various traditions. Egyptian flavouring may inform the solar imagery, although here
is a 'sun' that outclasses the 'wild old lion' Atum-re (the sun god, 12.9).
Some have made much of the zodiacal implications of Joseph's 12 light-
rays and precious stones, but 12 is of course an important image for
Israel. Moreover, close at hand is the biblical imagery of the 'chariot',
associated with Elijah (2 Kgs 2.11-12), with God's *shekina* (Ezek. 1.4-28
et passim) and with the light of the sun in Psalm 19 (or more specifically,
Ps. 18 LXX). In this Psalm, the sun comes forth out of his chamber as a
bridegroom, pursuing a course in heaven, and inescapable in the effect of
his warmth. The Greek version of this Psalm may in fact be read as if the
sun itself is God's tabernacle (*skēnōma*, v. 5), where God dwells, an interpretation consonant with Joseph's title 'Son of the Living God'. Joseph,
then, personifies the sun as a moveable shrine of God: he is possessed by
God's 'spirit' and 'grace' (4.7) and can divinely pierce the dark with light
(*Aseneth* 6.6; cf. Ps. 139.7). Calumnious words against Joseph amount to
blaspheming God himself (13.13). With Joseph comes the glory and the
mercy of the Almighty. The outstretched *and budding* olive branch in
Joseph's right hand suggests clemency, beneficence and the anointing
power of God's agent. Joseph's aspect outshines that of Aseneth for the
moment, as Israel outshines pagan piety. We are reminded also of the
contrast between beloved and lover in the the Song of Solomon, where
the bridegroom is 'all radiant and ruddy' (5.10), while the Shulammite is
comely 'but dark' (1.5). Joseph matches Aseneth as bridegroom matches
bride, yet he also contrasts with her in significant ways.

Aseneth's own appearance throughout this section likewise recalls
erotic imagery in the Song of Solomon. Besides combining features of
Wisdom and the strange woman, the description alludes to Song 4.12-
13, 15: 'a garden locked is my sister, my bride, a garden locked, a
fountain sealed. Your channel is an orchard of pomegranates, with all
choicest fruit… A garden fountain, a well of living water.' Aseneth,
surrounded by her paradisal courtyard, and bestowed with ripe fruit by
her parents while dressed in bridal attire, is just such an enclosed garden. Her utter seclusion adds to the marvel that her fame has spread so
widely, for 'no man had ever seen her'—until Joseph's keen eye sees
her leaning from the upper floor! Perhaps her nurtured beauty is

inferred by her admirers from the paradisal lushness of the courtyard garden, with which the scene closes:

> And handsome trees of all sorts and all bearing fruit were planted within the courtyard along the wall. And their fruit was ripe, for it was the time of harvest. And there was in the court, on the right hand, a spring of abundant living water, and below the spring was a big cistern receiving the water of that spring. From there a river ran right through the court and watered all the trees of that court (2.11-12).

Or, perhaps her charm has been blown to her beloved on the winds, as the parallel section in the Song of Solomon concludes: 'Awake, O north wind, and come, O, O south wind! Blow upon my garden that its fragrance may be wafted abroad. Let my beloved come to his garden and eat its choicest fruits' (Song 4.16).

The irony in *Aseneth* is that neither the beloved nor the lover are at the onset aware of their own desires, nor of the time that is fully ripe. The season in *Aseneth* differs pointedly from the *potential* fruitfulness suggested by the Song of Solomon's springtime (2.11-15; 6.11-12; 7.11-12), which is mirrored by the suggestive refrain, 'I adjure you...do not stir up or awaken love until it is ready' (1.7; 3.5). Song of Solomon employs breast imagery in order to suggest immaturity, or (alternately) readiness for erotic love: 'your breasts are like two fawns' (4.5; 7.3); 'may your breasts be like clusters of the vine...let us see whether the vines have budded' (7.8, 12); 'we have a little sister, and she has no breasts' (8.8); 'my breasts were like towers' (8.10). There is no similar dispute concerning Aseneth's prepared state, although there is a development of sorts: when she comes to greet Joseph, 'her breasts were already standing upright like handsome apples' (8.5); by the time that her recreation is fully accomplished, she will be transformed so that her breasts 'are like the mountains of the Most High God' (18.9). All the imagery and setting of the story, plus the familial and benedictory words of Joseph, signal to the reader what the characters do not seem to grasp: this marriage, and this joining of Aseneth to the Almighty, is inevitable. It seems that what has been dismissed as mere erotica in the longer version (the breast imagery) connects the work more closely with its biblical intertexts, and also creatively links the erotic and the spiritual. Aseneth's description matches both her receptivity to Joseph and her spiritual condition, as befits a story that is both a romance and a tale of conversion or spiritual transformation. Whether the imagery is completely sober, or whether there is an element of play in some of this (as there seems to be in the Song of Solomon) is a question worth considering. The treatment of characters and imagery thus leads to a discussion of discourse and tone.

Discourse and Tone

Subtlety and irony are sometimes in the eye of the beholder. It is much more easy to pick up direct 'messages' than to determine those that are more nuanced. This is true of *Aseneth*, where proper behaviour is, from time to time, unequivocally articulated, and therefore easily discernible. The first instance of this occurs (surprisingly) at a climactic moment (9.5-7), so that the reader's expectations of the couple's embrace is frustrated—the kiss will be suspended for several chapters! Instead Joseph goes on at length regarding 'what is fitting' for a God-fearer; his discourse extends beyond the needs of the narrative (i.e. to explain the ethos of a God-fearing man) to detail what is fitting for a God-fearing woman. His colourful discourse employs contrasting themes of idolatry and faithfulness to God, of life and death, of immortality and 'ambush', of incorruptibility and destruction. Here too are emphasized the themes noted in the first chapter, relating to kinship and strangeness. There is, however, a dissonance between his overt statement—in which Joseph implies that Aseneth is 'strange' and not 'his sister'—and the previous dialogue between Joseph and Pentephres, in which Aseneth has been named 'like a sister' by her father (7.7) and 'a sister' (7.8) by Joseph himself. Here, then, there are two messages being signalled, not exactly contradictory, but at least qualifying one of the other: purity and faithfulness are important; the boundaries between strange and kin are not impenetrable. The righteous and careful Joseph will not kiss; the meek and merciful Joseph utters a performative blessing, which immediately affects Aseneth. This mixed message is naturally echoed in Aseneth's mixed reaction (9.1). The attentive reader is called to perceive the complexity of life, without being induced to abandon all standards. This complexity is explained in theological terms by Joseph—God, the creator, can bring life to the dead (8.9).

This is a heavy message for a romance to bear. Yet there is a light touch as well. We have already noted the possible humour associated with the emphasis upon Aseneth's virginity—at the very least, this is an ambivalent trait, indicating alternately misandry and a valued chastity. It would seem that it is in the domestic scenes that humour is allowed to emerge. Is it employed in ch. 2, where we hear twice of 'aloneness' and the exclusion of even a male child? Perhaps. Is there a hint of it in ch. 4, where Aseneth takes issue with her father's wording, as an adolescent is wont to do?': 'Why does my lord and father speak such words as these, to *hand me over*, like a captive' (4.9; cf. 4.8). Or is there a nudge to the audience at 4.10, where Aseneth mistakenly associates Joseph's prophetic abilities with the magical practices of old wives? Certainly the interplay of narration, discussion between Joseph and Pentephres, and Joseph's remarks to himself, has a comic effect in ch. 7:

> Joseph was afraid, saying, 'This one must not molest me, too.'…
> And Joseph rejoiced exceedingly with great joy because Pentephres had said, 'She is a virgin hating every man.'
> And Joseph said by himself, 'If she is a virgin hating every man, this (girl) will certainly not molest me.'
> And Joseph said to Pentephres and his whole family, 'If she is your daughter and a virgin, let her come, because she is a sister to me, and I love her today as my sister' (7.3-8).

The formulaic reference to joy ('rejoiced exceedingly with great joy') is incongruous with the issue at hand. As we move on, the humour is unmistakable. My young listener, mentioned above, snickered at Joseph's self-consolation, with its formulaic tautology. The astute listener will go on to see the disparity between Joseph's inner reasoning and his receptive words to Pentephres. In fact, Joseph himself does not believe what he says to his host, but will come to own his own words. There is a knowing smile across the gulf between author and reader at this point.

Such lightness is the stuff of a beguiling story. Yet it does not, to my mind, have the effect of undercutting the serious ethical or theological concerns of *Aseneth*. We are accustomed, in our western culture, to dramas in which high and low characters come together to make a spectacle. Usually, the 'moral' of the story is embedded in the actions and discourse of the high characters, while the 'fabliau' or farcical characters add levity to the production. Even in western literature, this convention is not hard and fast, as those who learn from Shakespeare's fool or from Falstaff know. In *Aseneth*, we encounter a 'drama' where high and low are not separated, but mingled within two characters. This is perhaps the challenge in reading this piece: to determine at which points it functions at the level of a romance, or even a 'high mimetic' drama of courtly and noble characters, where it imitates life in a lower mode, and where it slips upwards into the mythical (stories about gods) or typological (where the natural affords a mould to understand the eternal). *Aseneth* seemingly follows the traditional hermeneutic applied to the Song of Solomon—God's love for his people—while retaining a literal and human level of love. To these two faces of spiritual and human intimacy, the narrative seemingly adds humour. The modern reader may be charmed or irritated by these breaches of modality. Is this conflation of modes the product of naïveté or of sophistication? Whatever our answer, it makes for complex and fascinating reading.

Plot and Structure

For a popular work, *Aseneth*'s structural devices are also intricate. We should note from the outset that the first section itself is structured as an *inclusio*. Chapter 1.1 begins with reference to Joseph's quest at the hands of Pharaoh, and his driving out on a particular day; 9.1 concludes the first scene with his intended departure, and promise to return. Scene one is thus initiated by Joseph's driving into Heliopolis, and ends with his driving out. Much has happened during Joseph's brief visit, despite the sense of stasis, and this is highlighted by the elements of the *inclusio* that do not quite match. Joseph arrives and leaves with a significant note about the date, but attention is now removed from the season, and placed upon the weekly count: it is the first day of the week, and more is promised when this day comes around again in cycle (9.1). Again, it is interesting to note that Pharaoh's function as initiator of a quest has now been largely displaced, except as a setting for the story. Joseph arrived on order of Pharaoh but leaves, with the intent to return, in imitation of a higher ruler, the Almighty creator, who can recreate. What has begun as a merely human story is being transmuted into something else, as will become clear in the next section.

The work induces a certain ethos by its intriguing imitation of biblical narrative, complete with biblicizing phrases, and even structural anomalies, such as doublets. For example, the action of 1.2 is stalled to give details of the key players, but is resumed with repetition of language at 3.1, giving the novel a Pentateuchal 'feel'—the same sense of 'seams' that led scholars towards source analysis. These devices, linked to the network of biblical intertextual echoes, sets up the romance as a piece with weighty subject matter. The mirroring and contrasting description of Joseph and Aseneth is also an important device that will be developed more fully in the sections that follow. This initial 'once upon a time' section has indicated, sometimes explicitly, and sometimes more subtly, *Aseneth*'s key concerns, and has done so in an engaging manner. Plot has been developed by the introduction of complication and intimated fulfilment so that we, like Aseneth, wait to see what will happen, and why this story has been written.

2. The Turning Point (Chapters 10-17)

Time, Space and Action

Chapter 10 begins with a contrast between the other characters, who depart, and Aseneth, who is left alone—with her virgins, but also in seclusion from them. The entire complex of chs. 10–17 provides the turning point of the first story, and takes place entirely within Aseneth's chambers. It is thus technically a time of stasis, as befits the 'liminal' status of the heroine. What action occurs takes place within the sacred seven-day period, and much of this time is spent in discourse, rather than action. Nevertheless, Aseneth's actions, and the actions of the Visitor from heaven, though spatially confined, are significant, and there is a sense in which their spatial confinement opens on to a vast world beyond the ordinary life of the actors. 'Timeful' rather than 'timeless' would be an apt description of this section.

Aseneth's first action, as the night falls, is to leave her upstairs sanctuary, go down to the gateway (of the tower?) and hurriedly remove the veil that hangs there as a door. In the light of the tower imagery that we have noted, the reminders of Burchard, Bohak and Kraemer are apt, that this unusual word for 'curtain' (*katapetasma*) is normally used for the temple veil. (See Burchard, *OTP*, II, p. 215 n. *h*; Bohak, *Joseph and Aseneth*, p. 70; and Kraemer, *When Aseneth*, p. 119.) The location of the curtain at the gateway to the entire tower complex is a little odd, however: why not directly outside Aseneth's chamber? We are, however, not dealing with allegory, but rather a story that utilizes a general notion of increasing seclusion, on the analogy of the 'graded holiness' (Bohak's term) of the temple. Much has been made of this detail, but at the very least we may say that Aseneth goes to great lengths—clandestinely removing the curtain so as not to wake the keeper—to remove a symbol of her seclusion. That she fills the object with ashes and hauls it back to her room, bolting the door behind her adds to the momentousness of the action. It could be that the curtain is merely a skin, and not made of the usual materials and colours for a holy veil, as a deliberate *contrast* to YHWH's temple. This would be consonant with the dishonour that it is now afforded, as it (along with the 'priestess' of idols and of her own virginity) is soiled with ashes. Again, the removal of this object is highly suggestive of Aseneth's change of demeanour, which from this point on evinces a vulnerable stance before the Almighty. Aseneth's door is bolted to her companions, but her window and 'temple' is opened to the One who can enter in another way.

The virgins awake briefly to show their solidarity and sympathy with their mistress, but are sent away and leave her in solitude.

There follows, for the prescribed time of seven days, a frenzy of mourning (cf. Gen. 50.10; Sir. 22.12) and contrition, which is to be understood as Aseneth's preparation for the revelation to come (cf. *4 Ezra* 5.13 *et passim; 2 Bar.* 9.2). Appropriately, she dons black garb, 'grinds' her idols in Mosaic repudiation, and rejects these, along with her riches, her food and other accoutrements, by throwing them out through the public north window. Aseneth's 'humiliation' is a time of mourning for her old life, of contrition and of preparation for what is to come. As the eighth day dawns, perhaps we expect immediate action: the sun is up, birds are singing, dogs are barking, people are passing. But Aseneth simply raises her head a little: we will bear, along with her, the stasis for a while longer. Action comes in stages, and with great effort, as she is tired not only in body but in spirit. Her first word is silent, and to herself, as she rehearses (with some hyperbole!) her penitent actions, and what she knows of the living and active God of Joseph. Her second speech is appropriately prefaced by an increased action of knees and hands, but again she cannot open her mouth. She muses upon the might of the Most High, but eventually takes courage in the prophetic promise that God is doubly active, healing those whom he chastises (11.10; cf. Isa. 30.26; Hos. 6.1). The third effort is successful, as she repeats her previous action, but finally also looks towards heaven and opens her mouth. Her third prayer is full of action imagery, detailing God's creative power and her spiritual 'flight' from idolatry to the Lord, and rehearsing her acts of contrition. The closing prayer, in fact, rounds off Aseneth's time of preparation, as we hear again of her penitent actions a week earlier (13.2-11) and flash back to her disrespect for Joseph—the crown of her sins. Aseneth's parting words confer a tentative benediction of Joseph (13.15), one that corresponds in a pale way to the blessing that he had given to her (8.9).

As she falls silent, Aseneth becomes aware of the 'great day' because heaven acts: the morning star arises, light appears, heaven is torn apart, and a figure from heaven comes to stand by her head, calling her. Much, though not all, of the action that follows is initiated and commanded by this figure. Aseneth herself initiates several actions—her self-veiling is rejected, but her provision of a table (accompanied by the touching of the Visitor's knees! [15.14]) and the final request to bless her seven virgins are received. The actions of the Visitor in this section are naturally all directed towards the revelation of mysteries. As Aseneth has 'revealed' (*apokalypso*, 12.3) her sins to God in her preparatory time, so now mysteries have been revealed to her (*apekalyphthē*, 16.14). Time is suspended, or perhaps taken up into eternity, as Aseneth's (and our) gaze is fixed upon the denizens of the heavens, upon what is written from eternity in God's book, upon the central mystery of the Visitor's name, and upon the significance of the honeycomb and the bees. However, human time is not entirely forgotten—especially in the longer version, which accentuates this time reference—as we hear of what will happen from 'today' (15.5, 10; 16.16). The final mystery of the honeycomb and the bees opens into Aseneth's own world, and the world of others who will follow her, as does her new name, 'City of Refuge', with which the revelation of the long version ends (17.6). The heavenly being departs, his chariot action reminiscent of Joseph's departure in the last scene. His visit, his mysterious actions, and his return have taken place in a time of 'rest' for Aseneth, a 'rest' that is promised to last forever to all who are the chosen of that city.

Characters and Imagery

Within this section these are, as we have seen, both intriguing and controversial. Aseneth marks the two stages of her transformation, humiliation and reception of blessing by changing her clothing. As she has imposed ashes, made mud with tears and fasted, she later removes her ashes (14.12), washes face and hands with living water, and will be fed. The used robe of mourning (10.9) is exchanged for a particular and untouched linen robe, and a twin girdle of virginity. Aseneth receives the Visitor's words with an unveiled face, indicative of her liminal state and receptivity that are apparently unhampered by her gender: later, though in a transformed state, she will resume the veil as part of her 'normal' but new life. While symbolic, the physical description at 14.14–15.1 is not belaboured, for the narrative is moving towards a superlative description of Aseneth's blessing, when she receives honeycomb from the Visitor:

> Behold, you have eaten bread of life, and drunk a cup of immortality, and been anointed with ointment of incorruptibility. Behold, from today your flesh will flourish like flowers of life from the ground of the Most High, and your bones will grow strong like the cedars of the paradise of delight of God, and untiring powers will embrace you, and your youth will not see old age, and your beauty will not fail for ever. And you shall be like a walled mother-city of all who take refuge with the name of the Lord God, the king of the ages (16.16).

Aseneth, the locked garden, is here *verbally* transformed into a walled city; the virgin is pronounced a mother. The short version never reaches this critical verification of Aseneth's new status, but Aseneth must simply trust the initial brief declaration of the messenger (15.6*P*). In the long version, the Visitor's promise is confirmed at the eating of the honeycomb, although not actually fulfilled. Nevertheless, the description at 16.16, with its many allusions to the Song of Solomon, corresponds strikingly to the transformative language that will be used at Aseneth's actual *metamorphosis* in ch. 18. That this is delayed in the longer version is no mistake, as we shall see. We should note, too, that this proleptic description of the new Aseneth includes the references to strong bones and untiring powers that are missing from Aseneth's cameo reflection in the water—so much for the suggestion that this is an inactive heroine, congenial to patriarchal tastes!

Aseneth's Visitor is described in terms that intensify the sun and chariot imagery used for Joseph. We have seen already that he gives a self-identification that links him to angelic orders, but no name. Something niggles here: our young reader asks, 'But who is he?' Perhaps the confusion arises because of echoes with the mysterious 'man' encountered by both Daniel and Ezekiel (8.2-4). In the LXX of Daniel and the initial description in Ezekiel, the same word *anthrōpos* is used. (Ezek 8.2 LXX supplies 'like a man [*anēr*]' where the Masoretic text says, 'like fire'):

> And Aseneth raised her head, and saw, and, behold, (there was) a man [Greek, *anthrōpos*] in every respect similar to Joseph, by the robe and the crown and the royal staff, except that his face was like lightning, and his eyes like sunshine, and the hairs of his head like a flame of fire of a burning torch, and hands and feet like iron shining forth from a fire, and sparks shot forth from his hands and feet (*Aseneth* 14.9-10).

> I looked up and saw a man (LXX *anthrōpos*) clothed in linen, with a belt of gold from Uphaz around his waist. His body was like beryl, his face like lightning, his eyes like flaming torches, his arms and legs like the gleam of burnished bronze, and the sound of his words like the roar of a multitude (Dan. 10.5-6).

> Seated above the likeness of a throne was something that seemed like a human form (LXX, *anthrōpos*). Upward from what appeared like the loins I saw something like gleaming amber, something that looked like fire enclosed all around; and downward from what looked like the loins I saw something that looked like fire, and there was a splendour all around... This was the appearance of the likeness of the glory of the LORD (Ezek. 1.27-28).

> I looked, and there was a figure that looked like a human being (LXX, *anēr*; corrected in NRSV on analogy with Ezek. 1?), below what appeared to be its loins it was fire, and above its loins it was like the appearance of brightness, like gleaming amber (Ezek. 8.2-4).

The mystery of Aseneth's Visitor, central to the structure of the long version, is compounded by these intertextual allusions, and the first person discourse as he announces Aseneth's acceptance. Who is 'the likeness of the glory of the LORD' (Ezek. 1.28); who is 'the chief of the house of the LORD' (*Aseneth* 14.8); who is this one who is 'like Joseph, except...' (*Aseneth* 14.4)? Is this figure glorified man, angel or otherwise? The story will not say, only hint and leave an unspoken mystery: 'Why do you seek this, my name, Aseneth?' (15.12x). Many exegetes have been uncomfortable letting the mystery be: many assume that the Visitor is Michael; others downplay the angelic allusions, stressing affinities with God's glory; some make this even more explicit, appealing to Metatron. In fact, no name is given, and this is greatly stressed in the long version. Readers should learn from the response of the chastened and now wise Aseneth, who, like Job, responds with closed mouth in ambiguous unspoken word: 'I did not know (a) god [God?] came to me... Be gracious, Lord...because I have spoken...all my words in ignorance' (17.9-10). To know that there is mystery is, it would seem, a revelation in itself, indeed the greatest secret that Aseneth has been afforded. Our young reader hears of the chariot ride away to the heavens and queries again, 'But who *is* he?'

The discussion of characters and imagery is incomplete without a consideration of the enigmatic 'bees', who dress in a manner uncannily like the hero and heroine: white, purple, violet, scarlet, gold-woven linen and gold diadems (16.18). Like Joseph (and his brothers in the second tale), they carry instruments of power, but 'harm no one'; like Aseneth, they eat from the honeycomb. Their place of origin from the honeycomb itself, their goal to build and eat from a comb on Aseneth's mouth, and their ultimate resting place heaven (or, for the vicious bees, Aseneth's garden) are no doubt significant, but difficult to interpret. The imagery of the honeycomb is the most evident feature, and recalls again Psalm 19 (18 LXX), which was key in the description of the sun-like Joseph. Honeycomb, precious breath from God's mouth, and equal to life-giving bread, immortal cup and incorruptible ointment, has fed Aseneth, and in this sequence her mouth becomes the source of nourishment, in a kind of symbiotic relationship with these mysterious bees. God's law, no doubt understood here through Sir. 24.20 in terms of wisdom, is sweeter than honey from the comb, making the simple wise (Ps. 19.10, 7).

The bee-encircled Aseneth in this enacted sign both benefits others and is protected from those that would hurt her, eventually giving suc-

cour to them as well (16.23). Gideon Bohak's interpretation of these
bees as priestly is intriguing, but the multitude of these creatures, and
their parallels with Joseph's brothers, seem to suggest a more general
allusion. We may also point to Israel's Deuteronomic blessing of
Joseph, where Aseneth's offspring, Menasseh and Ephraim, are said to
spawn 'myriads' and 'thousands' (Deut. 33.17). Could this scene suggest the interrelationship between Gentile converts to the Lord and the
original 'kingdom of priests' (Exod. 19.6), which both nourishes and
receives nourishment from an enlightened Gentile community, as the
prophetic literature sometimes envisions (cf. Isa. 61.5-7; 65.18-21)?
This understanding does not require the intricate symbolism of a rival
temple and priesthood, such as suggested by Bohak, nor his unlikely
interpretation of the offered honeycomb (17.3) as the destruction of the
temple in Jerusalem. Moreover, if the vision suggests such a scenario,
then we can also make sense of the anomalous bees, who 'would not
injure anyone' but subsequently 'wanted to hurt Aseneth' and were
thwarted. The bees' hostility appears within the vision–sign as an aber-
ration, quickly corrected; in the light of the events of chs. 22–29, its
signalled abnormality may indicate the author's discomfort with contemporary strained relations in the 'household of God'.

Discourse and Tone
Throughout chs. 10-17 the discursive tone is solemn and charged with
meaning. Gone are the domestic touches or the irony of the first section, or even its practical moralism. Where extended speech in the first
section (e.g. Joseph's words regarding 'what befits a God-fearer') tends
often towards deliberative instruction, the discourse in this central section is characterized by *encomia*, or praises. Reference to 'blessing' and
to what is 'blessed' because of contact with God permeate the
epiphany; the joy of Aseneth at the messenger's words (15.11) is recip-
rocated by the messenger, who appreciates her ability to receive these
mysteries so gladly and with such awe (16.12-14) This rhetorical mode
of celebration fits well with the mystery of chs. 14-17, for the biblical
pattern joins revelation with fear, then praise. Within the narrative,
Aseneth's penitential speeches are deliberative, for they function to
embolden her appeal to God. Nevertheless, close analysis demonstrates
that they exhibit strong affinities with the *encomium* as well: the excellence of the Almighty is their central theme. As these are lengthy, and
more mixed in mode, a rhetorical analysis of the shorter and 'purer'
discourse on Metanoia (15.7-8) may serve better to demonstrate the

general atmosphere and tendency that runs throughout the section. We compare the elements of the Visitor's instruction to the typical elements of the *encomium*, as it was prescribed in classical rhetoric:

> *Introduction*: Repentance is in the heavens (15.7)
> *Narration* (Origin/Genealogy/Birth) a good daughter of the Most High (15.7)
> *Achievements*
> > *Education* is omitted
> > *Virtues*: beauty, pure, laughing, gentle meek (15.7, 8)
> > *Deeds*: oversees virgins, mediates with God, prepares a place of rest (15.7-8)
> > *Blessings/Endowments*: God's love, angels' awe [Visitor's love] (15.8)
> *Conclusion*
> > *Honour/Memorial* (only implied): therefore peoples are welcome to join themselves to God in her name.

The fit is almost exact, and works well within the vision report, since the *encomium* develops through narration. Attention to what is omitted or transmuted also helps to disclose the particularities of this piece, and its special affinities with biblical sensibilities. First, it is important to note that, especially in the longer version, whatever praise is suggested for Metanoia is ultimately directed, throughout the passage, towards her 'Father'. This careful redirection is consonant with the observation of some rhetorical analysts that biblical argumentation may not easily draw upon this mode of speech. Contrived arguments encouraging the praise of God seem presumptuous; outright *encomia* of lesser beings seems extravagant. This problem is not insurmountable, however, in the case of a personified quality (i.e. Metanoia). In the introduction, the ideal quality of Repentance is given: she is 'in the heavens'. Her origin follows, as expected, paralleling the biblical descriptions of Wisdom. However, her training or education is not highlighted, since the eternal quality of this 'daughter' is essential. The Visitor's words would not be strengthened by the need to establish the job-readiness of this overseeing character! Contrary to the usual pattern, Metanoia's deeds are generally detailed before her virtues, a feature that points to the function of this passage—to show why Metanoia is significant for humankind. Towards the end of the praises, the discourse turns back towards the story-line: the last 'endowment' (the mysterious speaker's love of Metanoia) hints at the coming relationship between Aseneth and Joseph. Again, there is no concluding call to praise or even to join Metanoia, as we might have expected. This makes sense within the story, since Aseneth has already made this move. Moreover, an overt appeal to the reader is supplanted by the Visitor's assurance of love for Aseneth and those who follow her ('because she loves you virgins, I love you [plural] too'). The final message moves away from praise, then, to the encouragement of those who recognize Metanoia as praiseworthy. The blessing that is being enacted in Aseneth's encounter with the heavenly Visitor is extended, rather transparently, to the world outside the text. A similar move is made in the appendix-like blessing of the seven virgins, with which the epiphany closes.

Plot and Structure
We have already discussed the chiastic structure of chs. 14–17 in the comparison of long and short texts. There, the revelation was seen to revolve around an undisclosed mystery. This feature is extremely significant in that it militates against an easy 'decoding' of this section into a series of symbolic visions with a patent message. Always, the living quality of a narrative—especially a vision-report—needs to be appreciated, or the images are tamed, as they are translated into propositional or deliberative language. The omission of a conclusion in the near-perfect encomium on Metanoia is also indicative of this allusive quality in visionary literature. While other parts of *Aseneth* tend towards didacticism or deliberation, the central section is much more subtle, omitting direct paraenesis in a manner that is common in actual apocalypses. Even the questions answered by this section spawn a multitude of new ones. The Visitor is 'the chief of the house of the Lord'—but what is his name? Aseneth will be a 'City of Refuge'—but what exactly does that mean? She is fed with honeycomb—but how is that a blessed bread, cup and anointing? She is mother to many—but to whom, exactly, and in what sense? She receives unutterable mysteries—can her 'children' expect to do that too? Everywhere the narrative leaves trails, spinning away from the more obvious messages that it delivers: that repentance is key to living, that God reveals secrets to those who are loved, that God joins the faithful together; that God's ways and mysteries are unsearchable.

3. 'Happily Ever After' (Chapters 18–21)

Time, Space and Action
Time again speeds up as the third and final section of the first tale follows hard on the heels of the central revelatory section. Aseneth is interrupted when a servant arrives, announcing the return of Joseph in words that echo his first arrival: 'Behold, Joseph the Powerful One of God is coming to us today (18.1; cf. 3.1). The story of Aseneth and

Joseph's meeting is about to be retold, again at a fast tempo, but with a difference. In the first part, the scene was set, marriage proposed and refused, Joseph arrived to be entertained and Aseneth entered into mourning. After her confession and visitation from heaven, Joseph arrives again, is entertained in a common meal, they are married and the scene is put in a larger context (Egypt). What has happened to Aseneth has removed the obstacles introduced in the first section. The inner atmosphere of prayer and vision in chs. 10–17 is thus surrounded by the intrigue and action of chs. 1–9 and 18–21. Before this resolving action actually resumes, however, there is still a part of Aseneth's transformation to be accomplished. Now the 'static' heroine has been freed to take action, and her action is of utter significance, especially as related in the long version.

The Delayed Transformation. What has been pronounced in the vision sequence, Aseneth's new identity, is now fulfilled, as Aseneth puts into action the instructions of the Visitor (15.10-11). Until she responds actively to his command, dressing as the one whom she is to become, the transfer is incomplete. This is in fact underscored by the observations of her 'foster-father', who sees only a weary penitent. Aseneth, as before, 'hurries' into her second chamber to dress, and then intends to do something about her 'fallen face'. It is unnecessary, for as she leans over to wash it, she is startled by her reflection: not only is she glorious with beauty, she has taken on the vastness of a strong and protected land of God: fields, vegetation, fighting men, protective mountains (18.8). This 'City' of refuge is expansive and awesome, and is responded to appropriately by the foster-father, who declares, 'At last the Lord God of heaven has chosen you'.

The transformation of Aseneth, then, follows three major stages, all of which take place in the shelter of Aseneth's own chambers. At the first stage, her contrition and three-fold prayer comprises an inner transformation, preparatory for what is to happen. This stage is symbolized by her black dress and solitude, and corresponds to the first initiation rite of separation, in anthropological studies. Next, her experience with the man (*anthrōpos*), a liminal state, involves the hearing of mysteries and the pronouncement of her new status within the sacred community. This stage is symbolized by the 'distinguished' dress that she dons, and the open face with which she receives these things. Now, in ch. 18, her aggregation into the new life is complete, as she is declared a bride. The completion is clinched by her change of clothing (bridal, with seven jewels), by her physical transformation, by the unembarassed presence of another male figure, by his stationary amazement for 'a long time' and by pronouncement. Certainly this delayed transformation complicates the action of Aseneth, but it is not haphazard. No aggregation can fully occur in a secluded liminal setting. Aseneth must leave extraordinary 'sacred' space (chs. 14–17) and re-enter her world, taking the blessing with her; her world, as well as her being, are to be transformed.

The Narrative Resumes. The unhindered progress of time and action is signalled by a second announcement: 'Behold, Joseph is standing at the doors of our court' (19.1; cf. 5.1). Presumably the family is away again, enjoying their usual freedom, for Aseneth is left to answer the door. Only at this point in the story does the heroine venture 'outside of the entrance' (though still within the guarded courtyard) to meet Joseph. The other virgins, who wait by the entrance, presumably are less prepared for such freedom (19.2-4). Her liberty, which is detailed only in the long version, is mirrored also in the lengthy conversation that follows. Joseph is now overthrown by beauty, and must ask Aseneth to interpret the mystery of her own identity. The actions that follow are mutual and balanced. Both speak in dialogue, both stretch out hands, both wrap arms around the other and interlock hands. Joseph is now invited into *her* and *our* house, and Aseneth returns kisses with him—there is no separate table, but total integration. This mutual activity is sustained until the scene with Pharaoh, as in marriage he joins them mouth to mouth. Joseph does not at this point 'kiss' Aseneth, but they kiss each other. The freedom of action is mirrored by the freedom of place—Joseph can freely go in to Aseneth's house (and in the final verse, 21.9, 'in to Aseneth'); Aseneth can leave her courtyard, go before Pharaoh and finally leave her father's protective custody. The freedom of movement is accentuated by the enlarged setting of the conclusion, 'the whole land of Egypt *and all the kings of the nations*' (21.8). Aseneth's fame as a bride has spread even farther than the renown she possessed as a virgin.

Characters and Imagery
Intricate descriptions of characters and images are found even in this faster-paced third section, although far less frequently in the shorter version. Aseneth's seven jewels and her royal sceptre are strong images of her newly fulfilled identity. Her transformed appearance as a bride, and Joseph's recognition of her as 'City of Refuge' balance and com-

plete the descriptions which have preceded this section. Of real significance is the first embrace of the couple (which is marked by mutuality in the long version) as well as the blessing of Aseneth, who receives 'spirit of life', 'wisdom' and 'truth' in a threefold kiss. This embrace corresponds to the triple blessing over Aseneth's head, and confirms the resolution of the action.

All the images in this section are tinged with light, infused with life, and studded with riches: 'lightning' (18.5), 'sun...and morning star', 'rose of life' (18.9), 'walls of life' (19.8), 'like appearance of light' (20.6), 'life to the dead' (20.7), 'golden crowns' (21.6) 'conception... and birth (21.8). Aseneth's concluding confessional psalm (21.10-21) recaps the progress of the story from darkness to light, from death to life and from spiritual poverty to riches. Intimately connected with these images of light, life and riches is the theme of wisdom, laced into the narrative by phrases and words such as 'fast-writing scribe', 'spirit', 'since eternity' and 'from the beginning and of old'.

Discourse and Tone

The tone of this concluding section is intriguing, bringing together the various moods of the drama—solemnity, awe, excitement, some moralism and (while irony has been abandoned) even a little humour. The paraenetic flavour that we noted in the first section, and which will come to the fore in the second tale (chs. 22–29) emerges at one point, where Joseph declares what is 'not fitting' for the betrothed before their marriage (21.1). Interestingly, this verse also fulfils the promise of Joseph that he will, on the eighth day, actually lodge with his host—but this sojourn is to be short-lived, as there is urgent business at hand. For the rest of the sequence, the instruction or 'messages' are far more subtle, and achieved through a combination of styles. One short interchange, 19.4-9. demonstrates these jostling moods. Here is the sequence:

Setting:	Joseph amazed at Aseneth
Question:	'Who are you? Tell me quickly'
Aseneth:	Rehearsal of experience, embedded oracle
Joseph:	Benediction and Pronouncement
Question:	'Why do you stand far away from me?

This sequence moves from awe, through excited questioning, through the serious rehearsal of Aseneth's apocalypse, and closes firmly with Joseph's solemn benediction—only to be lightened by Joseph's question! On hearing it, the reader remembers Joseph's earlier repudiation of Aseneth's embrace and smiles. It is as if Joseph, late himself on the uptake, is quip-

ping, 'What took you so long?' His invitation is parallel to the 'at last'
comment of the foster-father. Most readers will be similarly relieved!
This light touch does not, however, undercut Joseph's joyful benediction (19.8-9), a discourse that rounds off the action and presses home a
theological perspective. Aseneth is blessed *because* God has established
her, and because she now has a role to play in the nurturing of those
over whom God will reign (19.9). As in the description of Metanoia,
praise for Aseneth is transmuted into praise for the Almighty. The contemporary reader is left, however, wondering about Aseneth's 'sons'
(19.8) and their relation to Manasseh and Ephraim. Kraemer (*When
Aseneth*, p. 184 n. 161) intimates the possibility of Samaritan interest in
Aseneth's pedigree, since the Samaritan community traced their lineage
from these two half-tribes. Equally plausible is an eschatological scenario
in the mind of the author, particularly considering the future tense and
eternal aspect of Joseph's benediction. Does the story conceive of a
future time where all who turn to the Most High, whether penitent Jew,
of the lost tribes, or transformed Gentile, will dwell in a place of refuge
and peace?

Aseneth, by virtue of her union with Joseph, and her conception of
the twins, is an apt symbol of this future hope. Perhaps, in concert with
the prophet (Isa. 66.18-23), *Aseneth* envisages a time when the
Deuteronomic 'first-born bull' Joseph with his two horns (Deut. 33.17)
will be tamed, no longer driving the peoples to the ends of the earth,
but calling them into one household, as suggested by the compass-trac-
ing finger of the man (*anthrōpos*) of God. Then, not only will Joseph,
but all of Aseneth's offspring taste 'the choice gifts of heaven…the
choice fruits of the sun…the finest produce of the ancient mountains'
(Deut. 33.13-15). In the words of Aseneth, 'the gifts of your inheritance, Lord, are incorruptible and eternal' (12.15). Aseneth's own closing psalm confirms this beneficence, closing with the gifts of the Most
High—bread of life, cup of wisdom and intimacy with the people of
God (21.21).

Plot and Structure
The structure of this final section, as a conclusion to the first narrative, is
coherent only in terms of an overview of the book's overall structure.
We have noticed already the overall three-fold structure of *Aseneth*, and
seen intimations of its chiastic structure, both in smaller units and more
generally. The 'apocalypse' or revelatory sequence of chs. 14–17 provides the centre of the first tale, with its unsolved mystery of the mes-

senger's name at the utter centre. However, the epiphany is also integrally connected to Aseneth's seven days of preparation (chs. 10–13) and
to her physical transformation in ch. 18. Thus, chs. 10–18 are together a
time of earthly stasis; as a time of mystic and spiritual activity, they also
comprise the turning point of the plot. Chapter 18 is a link chapter,
enacting the promised transformation of Aseneth, and also merging into
the resumed narrative, because of its aggregative character. In the longer
version, the significance of Aseneth herself, and the mystery surrounding her, are placed slightly off-centre, so that the reader's attention is
ultimately focused upon the action, being and mystery of the Most
High. Even the pagan Pharaoh, who cannot yet speak of 'my God' but
'Jacob's God' blesses in the name of the unseen ordainer. (We may
wonder why a non-Hebrew officiates, but the story is confined by the
biblical narrative [cf. Genesis 41.45]. The narrative has worked hard,
through father imagery, to present Pharaoh as a kind of proxy for the
Almighty). The overall action of the first narrative thus assumes a balanced structure:

I   *Story Initiated* (1–9):
    A Setting of Heliopolitan home (1–2)
    B With father, refused marriage (3–4)
    C Joseph's light (5–6)
    D Feast set apart (7)
    E No kiss, three-fold prayer (8)
    F Aseneth in solitude (9)
II *Preparation* and inward transformation of the penitent (10–13)
III *Apocalypse*: Declaration of her transformation (14–17)
IV *Confirmation* and outward transformation (18)
V   *Story Fulfilled* (19–21.9)
    F′ Aseneth, Joseph, virgins secluded (19.3)
    E′ Threefold kiss (19.10)
    D′ Integrated feast (20)
    C′ Aseneth's brightness (20.6-8)
    B′ With father, marriage postponed and enacted (20–21)
    A′ Setting enlarged, all of Egypt, Joseph's house (21.8-9)
    Interpretative Prayer (21.10-21)

This chiastic structure may be further filled out and explained through
attention to details in dress, repeated imagery, attention to food and feast-
ing, and key repeated words. (See Humphrey, *The Ladies*, pp. 40-51, for
further discussion of the chiastic features and balance of *Aseneth*.) Here is
a work of unusual character that brings together—usually in a sophisticated manner, but sometimes less smoothly—diverse rhetorical patterns
and literary structures. The hosting of an epiphany and unsolved mystery

within a romance is unique, and this peculiarity is matched by the work's unusually diverse rhetoric—at times direct, and bordering on the pedantic, but more often elusive and engaging. The search for an eschatological meaning to Aseneth's new status, such as I have attempted, should never stop in an impasse that claims to 'solve' *Aseneth*'s riddle. Before us remain lively and jostling themes, voices and concepts that should not be deadened by interpretation. In the end, *Aseneth* must be enjoyed.

4. Sequel or Afterthought? (Chapters 22–29)

Chapters 22–29 confirm this impression concerning Aseneth as a romance-with-a-difference. Our young listener, on reaching the end of the first tale, asks quizzically, 'But what about Pharaoh's son?' As with most good stories, the plot leaves space for a second tale. Not only are there hanging threads, but imagery and plot features that find their response in this sequel. Some readers, taken with the profound symbolism of the first story, are surprised by the breathless simplicity of the second. Yet the differences are only relative, as we shall see.

Time, Space and Action
As in the first tale, it 'happens' after this, that the second takes its point of departure from Genesis 46, when Jacob and his family join his son Joseph in Egypt, settling in Goshen. The setting, a time of famine, is appropriate to the adversity that will strike our protagonists. We might expect to hear immediately about Joseph's business in distributing grain, but after setting and time have been given, family matters prevail. It is Aseneth herself who acts in the first place, announcing her pious intent to visit the patriarch—one 'like a father' to her and '[a] god'. Do old idolatrous habits die hard, or is Aseneth foreshadowing the amazing epiphany of Jacob that will follow? Joseph accompanies her for this trip, which is not described as a lengthy journey, despite the importance of the travel theme in the 'novel' form. Immediately the couple arrive in Goshen and are reunited with the patriarch. The narrative seems unconcerned about developing a travelling motif in this section, but is more insistent to show the full extent of Aseneth's integration and new pedigree. Thus, the scene is marked by vigorous actions and imagery—prostration, wrestling, stretching, grasping, eating and drinking—that point to the strength of Jacob, and of Aseneth, who is now his daughter. It is on the return visit that the disjuncture from home is emphasized, as they are escorted by the friendly brothers,

Simeon and Levi: danger has crept into the action. On the same trip (or at least outside of the safety of home) the agent of the impending conflict joins the story—what about Pharaoh's son, indeed?

The next two sections involve good and tarnished characters coming and going from Pharaoh's house, as he plots to destroy what God has done ('Thus it shall not be!' 23.1). The first encounter with Simeon and Levi involves a frankness, a masculine display of swords, and a contest of anger and meekness. The two brothers' swords, glory tinged, overwhelm Pharaoh's son, who falls as though before an epiphany. The second encounter, at night, describes the union of deception (Pharaoh's son) and envy (the brothers), and ends with a dire plot to destroy Joseph, his children and Pharaoh himself. An ambush, intruding upon the estate of Joseph and Aseneth, is prepared apace, its site painstakingly described (24.20). The overall plan, however, falls apart from the beginning, with an aborted attempt on Pharaoh, who is protected in an inner chamber, and the misgivings of Naphtali and Asher against Dan and Gad: Joseph and his beloved will be preserved in the coming action, as Joseph was during his siblings' infamous Genesis plot.

In ch. 26, Aseneth again initiates action, though reluctantly separated from the otherwise-engaged Joseph, and the ambush commences. Throughout the next scene, she flees, calls twice upon God, and intercedes (as an incarnation of Metanoia) for her repentant assailants. The allies of Joseph act in various ways: Levi in concert with Aseneth as merciful prophet, Benjamin as brave warrior, Simeon and the others as loyal and unmatched combatants. Joseph plays no part in the action at all. A thicket of reeds serves both as the locale of intrigue and of refuge for the culprits, while Aseneth's rescuers follow their course in full view. Interestingly, the last we hear of the evil brothers, they are still in the thicket, covered by Aseneth's clemency and Levi's wisdom: they never regain the stage to be reconciled. Rather, the weight falls on Levi's charity towards Pharaoh's son; Levi is himself the epitome of the book's ethic. The final action is that of greatness prostrating itself before wisdom and mercy: Pharaoh abandons his throne before the prospect of Levi, and blesses him. Levi had sought to gain Pharaoh's favour, and make him 'like our father' (29.4); in the end, Levi is revered by Pharaoh.

This overturning of roles—the triumph of mercy over revenge, the lifting up of the meek and the lowering of the proud—are the dominant motifs in this tale. Through a less-than-subtle rhetoric, they are evoked at every point of the action. This second story has served to put a now-integrated Aseneth into the vanguard; in the first tale, her role was less

initiating, more receptive. It is confidence in God, however, that is ultimately celebrated, not Aseneth's own character, nor even the virtuous
quest to revenge her honour. All heroism is relativized by the greater
virtues of clemency, and dependence upon God, who humbles the arro-
gant. Even the closing setting participates in the dynamic, as Joseph
becomes 'like a father' to Pharaoh's younger son (29.9), even after his
48-year regency. Technically, Joseph may still be second in the land; in
honour, he and his family are first. The story ends, as it began, in Egypt,
where the merciful rule of the Most High has been established—at least
in a relative way. No celebration, or eating and drinking, rounds off the
victory, as in the first narrative. Thus, there is an open-endedness of
sorts, as Joseph and his family continue to negotiate their place in a
strange land. The reader knows what will happen after Joseph dies, and is
perhaps reminded of the tentative nature of security prior to the final
'place of rest'.

Characters and Imagery
This section, in conformity to its active quality, does not engage in
full-blown description or intricate imagery, except in its initial presentation of Jacob, which features the same glorious beauty of Psalm 19
(18 LXX), seen earlier in Joseph and transferred to Aseneth. Jacob's
active nature, both physical and spiritual, are accentuated—an apt
introduction to the ensuing story. He is described, as the sun, like a
'giant' (*gigas*, 22.7; cf. Ps. 18.6 LXX) with thighs, calves and feet ready
for action. Even longevity is a symbol of strength rather than frailty.
Aseneth's clinging to him as 'one who has returned from fighting' foreshadows the struggle to come. In this second tale, the reader will
receive a novelistic presentation of the agony of life. This realism is,
however, softened by the 'sharp-sighted' prophecies of Levi, who sees
back to the strong foundation of the faithful, and forward, despite present troubles, to their 'place of rest' beyond (22.13).
    The 'good' characters of the story together present the qualities
envisaged for those who 'attach' themselves to the Lord. They work in
concert to keep the archetypal God-fearer Aseneth safe, in a potentially
hostile world. The story is replete with descriptions of interrelationships, detailing carefully who is allied with whom, who grasps whose
hand, who is weakened by envy or revenge of others, who has insight
into character, and so on. Joseph, though mostly absent from the narrative, himself is presented as busily beneficent in a time of famine (25.5;
26.4). His benevolence is contrasted with the self-consumed son of

Pharaoh, who covets Aseneth, and who announces at 25.2, 'I am going out to harvest (the vintage of) *my* new-planted vineyard' (a subtle allusion to Aseneth?). Gad and Dan's traitorous activity, though forgivable, is seemingly modelled on their dubious 'blessing' by Israel in Gen. 49.17 and 19—'Dan shall be a snake by the roadside, a viper along the path that bites the horse's heels…Gad shall be raided by raiders, but he shall raid at their heels.' This is, of course, precisely what happens to these two, who are used by Pharaoh's son to raid, and who sit by the side of the road ready to strike. The verse that separates the two Genesis oracles, Gen. 49.18, describes Aseneth's stance throughout the turmoil: 'I wait for your salvation, O LORD.'

Discourse and Tone

The tone of this section is more overtly didactic than the first story. While a nod is given to mystery (22.13), the major accent falls on what should and what should not be done by the God-fearer, underpinned by promises that God will vindicate the righteous. The refrain: 'it does not befit' occurs frequently, at 23.9, 23.11 and 29.3. Other injunctions about the behaviour and attitude to be followed by those who worship God are found at 23.12; 26.2; 28.7; 28.11; and 28.14. The final scene of Levi, Pharaoh's son and Pharaoh hammers the lessons home: do not repay evil for evil; God will reward the merciful.

Usually the instruction is given briefly, matching the vigorous unfolding of the plot. Levi, as befits the archetypal wise man, has two more extensive discourses, which unfold in more flamboyant rhetoric (23.10-14; 29.3-4). The first is interesting as a mix of 'deliberative' (i.e. persuasive of a certain course of action) and 'judicial' speech, as Pharaoh's son is confronted and Levi attempts to dissuade him from evil. It employs a kind of tortured logic, as a 'peaceful' character engages in two activities—demonstrating the wickedness of violence and contemplating the necessity of conflict. Comparison against the 'complete argument' is instructive. (On the species of rhetoric, and classical formats for speeches, see Burton L. Mack, *Rhetoric and the New Testament* [Minneapolis: Augsburg-Fortress, 1990]):

Introduction:	Ethos of Levi established ('frankness, his face cheerful') by manner; he establishes a link ('our lord') with Pharaoh's son (23.10)
Proposition:	A. It is wrong to contemplate violence and implicate others
	B This particular course of action is unwise (23.10b)
Reason.	A 'For' we worship God
	B And Joseph is our brother, and powerful (23.11)
Opposite	The one who would so act sins before God and Israel and brother

Example	A The God-fearer does not injure anyone
	B The God-fearer does not help someone who wants to do this
Citation?	'a sword is not in his hands' (23.12; cf. Rom. 12.4)
Conclusion	A So stop speaking this way
	B And if you don't our swords are in our hands! (23.13)

Except for the complicated and casuistic 'Example', the A phrases correspond to the judicial atmosphere (this is wrong), and the B phrases to the demonstrative (this is an unwise course of action). The conflict between judicial and demonstrative comes to the fore in the contrasting statements regarding the sword. We are reminded again of the sting-bearing bees, who would not hurt anyone. Strength, measured by reserve, is explicitly pronounced in the second tale, but only suggested in the first. The contradiction seems more apparent in this 'logically' argued sequence than in the symbolic mode of the apocalypse, which has more potential to hold contraries together.

Plot and Structure
Since the plot does not require a slowing of the action to host an epiphanic vision, the structure of the second tale does not mirror that of the first. There is no chiastic arrangement, although there is some correspondence between the beginning and end, particularly in the setting 'frames'. The story begins by introducing the protagonists within their family setting, and finishes by showing their relation with outsiders, so again there is some balance. However, the story moves towards its major climax about three-quarters of the way through (ch. 27.7), and then resolves quickly. Action continually builds from the complication foreshadowed at 22.11, during the description of the family (some of whom are hostile). Suspense increases as we hear of the envy of Pharaoh's son, his machinations with two groups of brothers, his preparations for the ambush, and the ambush itself, amazingly thwarted. There is a false climax, as Aseneth flies ahead from Pharaoh's son, calling out to God (26.8). The highest point of suspense is reached when a plot to abduct is intensified into an attempt to murder Aseneth. Aseneth's own discourse at the climax recalls God's promise of life (17.10). A final *deus ex machina* destroys the enemy's weapons (a sword is truly not in their hands!) and the denouement deals with all the remaining complications: the repentance of the traitors, the adrenaline of the rescuers, the conflict of justice and mercy, the problem of Pharaoh's son. Peace and security are restored, with the wise man Joseph virtually in control. These dynamics are seen more easily in a graph:

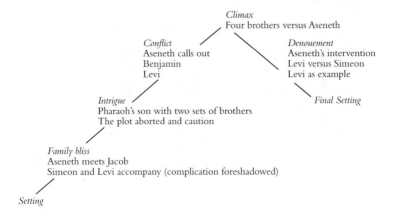

Climax
Four brothers versus Aseneth

Conflict
Aseneth calls out
Benjamin
Levi

Denouement
Aseneth's intervention
Levi versus Simeon
Levi as example

Intrigue
Pharaoh's son with two sets of brothers
The plot aborted and caution

Final Setting

Family bliss
Aseneth meets Jacob
Simeon and Levi accompany (complication foreshadowed)

Setting

Unlike the first story, which has a lengthy turning point, and is structured with careful equilibrium so as to place accent upon God's revelation to Aseneth, the second story builds inexorably to its climax, and then is quickly resolved. This is apt, since the first story introduces the eternal into the life of an archetypal figure at her point of liminality and transformation, whereas the second tale has a 'meanwhile' and didactic realism (despite its fabulous genre!). Put together, the stories conspire to convince the reader that Aseneth's greatest conflict and highest adventure were accomplished when she approached, and was met by, the Most High. Vicissitudes of life after that point may prove complex, but if the reader borrows the keen eyes of Levi, the courage of Aseneth and the meekness of both, they may be assured of preservation from harm and continual blessing. Times of famine will be met by the grain stored up in the years of plenty: the bread-giver Joseph exemplified this in times of yore. Thus are the bread of life, cup of wisdom and ointment of incorruptibility offered to those who, with Aseneth, anticipate their ordained place of rest.

Further Reading

On Vision and Rhetoric

Humphrey, Edith M., 'I Saw Satan Fall...'—The Rhetoric of Vision', *ARC* 12 (1993), pp. 75-78.

—'Collision of Modes?—Vision and Determining Argument in Acts 10.1–11.18', *Semeia* 71 (1995), pp. 65-84.

—'Why Bring the Word Down?—the Rhetoric of Demonstration and Disclosure in Romans 9.30–10.21', in S. Soderlund and N.T. Wright (eds.), *Paul's Letter to the*

Romans and the People of God (Festschrift Gordon Fee; Grand Rapids: Eerdmans, 1999).
—'In Search of a Voice: Rhetoric through Sight and Sound in Revelation 11.15–12.17', in L. Gregory Bloomquist and Greg Carey (eds.), *Vision and Persuasion: Rhetorical Dimensions of Apocalyptic Discourse* (St. Louis, MO: Chalice Press, 1999).
Mack, Burton L., *Rhetoric and the New Testament* (Minneapolis: Augsburg-Fortress, 1990). An indispensable beginner's guide to rhetorical analysis in biblical studies.
Robbins, Vernon K., 'Socio-Rhetorical Criticism: Mary, Elizabeth and the Magnificat as a Test Case', in Edgar V. McKnight and Elizabeth Struthers Malbon (eds.), *The New Literary Criticism and the New Testament* (Sheffield: Sheffield Academic Press, 1997), pp. 164–209. This essay gives an excellent introduction to Robbins's metacritical method, which seeks out the various 'textures' of a work: inner texture (analysis of the text itself), intertexture (the text alongside its implied comparative texts), social and cultural texture (the text in its world and the world at large), and ideological texture (the exploration of self-interests in the text and the reader). My aims are more modest, although we are both concerned to bring together various 'conversations' inherent in the text, and to consider 'new rhetoric' alongside more classical rhetorical studies. See also the introduction to his new edition of *Jesus the Teacher: a Socio-Rhetorical Interpretation of Mark* (Philadelphia: Fortress Press, 1992). His most thorough presentations of this method are found in two recent volumes: *The Tapestry of Early Christian Discourse: Rhetoric, Society and Ideology* (London: Routledge, 1996) and *Exploring the Texture of Texts* (Valley Forge, PA: Trinity Press International, 1996).
Watson, Duane F. and Hauser, Alan J., *Rhetorical Criticism of the Bible; A Comprehensive Bibliography with Notes on History and Method* (Biblical Interpretation Series, 4; Leiden: E.J. Brill, 1994). An indispensable aid for students interested in the evolution of rhetorical biblical criticism up to 1994.

Related Literature and Mythology

Charlesworth, James H., *The Old Testament Pseudepigrapha*, I (2 vols; ed. J.H. Charlesworth; Garden City, NY: Doubleday, 1983). This volume contains '*2 Enoch*', '*2 Baruch*' (2 versions), and 'The Martyrdom and Ascension of Isaiah', all of which feature journeys to the various spheres of heaven.
Eshel, E., Eshel, H., Newsom, C., Nitzan, B., Schuller, E., and Yardeni, A., in consultation with J.C. VanderKam and M. Brady, *Qumran Cave 4. VI. Poetical and Liturgical Texts, Part 1* (DJD, 11; Oxford: Clarendon Press, 1998). Official publication of Qumran material, in the ongoing DJD series. Of particular interest in this volume is section C, by Carol Newsom, which reproduces 4Q405, 4QShirot 'Olat HaShabbat, *Songs of the Sabbath Sacrifice*, Plates XXI–XXX.
Lichtheim, M. (trans.), *Ancient Egyptian Literature*, III (Berkeley University of California Press, 1980), III, pp. 134-35. Lichtheim translates the Demotic story of Setne-Khamwas and another Egyptian priest's daughter, Tabubu.
Newsom, Carol, *Songs of the Sabbath Sacrifice: A Critical Edition* (HSS, 27; Atlanta: Scholars Press, 1985), This new edition and commentary of the Qumran text is especially welcome. Pages 31-51 translate the portion that mentions the heavenly realms.

On Mimesis and Modes of Writing

Anderson, G., *Ancient Fiction: The Novel in the Greco-Roman World* (Totowa, NJ: Barnes & Noble, 1984). Anderson is particularly helpful in his emphasis upon the comic aspects of the ancient novel.

Black, Fiona, 'Unlikely Bedfellows: Feminist and Allegorical Readings of Song 7.1-8', in Athalya Brenner (ed.), *Feminist Companion to the Song of Songs*, II (Sheffield: Sheffield University Press, forthcoming). Black stresses the comic and grotesque aspect of erotic imagery in the Song of Solomon.

Frye, Northrop, 'Historical Criticism: Theory of Modes', in *idem, Anatomy of Criticism* (Princeton: Princeton University Press, 2nd edn, 1979 [1957]), pp. 33-67. An important and accessible essay that presents Frye's well-accepted theory of modes in literature.

Other Texts Cited in this Chapter

Bohak, Gideon, *Joseph and Aseneth and the Jewish Temple in Heliopolis* (Early Judaism and its literature, 10; Atlanta: Scholars Press, 1996).

Burchard, C., 'Joseph and Aseneth', in J.H. Charlesworth (ed.), *The Old Testament Pseudepigrapha*, II, pp. 177-247.

Humphrey, E.M., *The Ladies and the Cities: Transformation and Apocalyptic Identity in Joseph and Aseneth, 4 Ezra, The Apocalypse and The Shepherd of Hermas* (JSPSup, 17; Sheffield: Sheffield Academic Press, 1995).

Kraemer, Ross S., *When Aseneth Met Joseph: A Late Antique Tale of the Biblical Patriarch and his Egyptian Wife, Reconsidered* (New York: Oxford University Press, 1998).

4

CONCLUSION AND PROSPECTUS

So we come to the end of our reading, both of the secondary literature, and of *Aseneth* itself. The consideration of methods and analysis, with their great diversities, may lead some readers to concur with Ross Kraemer, who thus concludes her major study: 'Like the image of the chameleon, [*Aseneth*'s] texts tend to resemble whatever we lay them against, leaving me more and more resigned to our inability to pin the texts down to a particular interpretation and a particular context' (*When Aseneth*, p. 294). I hope, however, that the reading of the apocryphon itself has demonstrated that, alongside its marked polyvalence, *Aseneth* retains its own peculiar accent, and also a vibrant connection with the world that never dissolves into idealist categories. Perhaps the work resembles less the chameleon than the cat with nine lives, retaining its grounding in a first (somewhat elusive) setting, but taking on renewed significance in the contexts of subsequent readers. To note the many possibilities of a symbolic and complex text (or group of texts) is not the same thing as to assert an endless number of contradictory possibilities. Identity is too strong a concept in *Aseneth* for its character to be completely malleable in the critic's hands. There may be many right answers, but there are also some wrong ones; there may be inappropriate questions as well.

We may imagine an *Aseneth* come to life, surrounded by her zealous analysts, now in the throes of a personality disorder. Is she Jewish or Christian, Gnostic or merkavah mystic, sectarian or mainstream, of long or short recension, Egyptian, Syrian or Samaritan, of BCE origin, or well into the common era? Is she patriarchal or feminist, novelistic or mystical, for entertainment, edification or mystification? Such questions are significant, but in the course of analysis it may be discovered that the condition is in part the result of professional projection, and not inherent in the book itself. We live in an age that loves complexity, and that delights in numerous approaches. *Aseneth* may well be 'the most obscure and elusive text of the Old Testament Pseudepigrapha' (George Nickelsburg, on the jacket of Kraemer, *When Aseneth*); but it has spoken cogently, if mysteriously, to generations beyond its first readers. Moreover, it is a book that was read, it seems, by less-than-sophisticated readers. Much still remains to be done in the area of text-critical study, the investigation of *realia* in the book, and the determination of the book's dating, purpose(s) and first setting. While noting continued difficulties here (*Aseneth* resolutely retains her condition of bookish amnesia), I have argued for a reasonable working hypothesis: *Aseneth* is a Jewish Hellenistic work (though congenial to some Christian communities) roughly dating from the two centuries surrounding the turn of the eras, best represented by the eclectic text of Burchard and well characterized as a romance with mystical and apocalyptic affinities. Students will have seen, however, that it is possible to learn much from those who take other positions.

In the pursuit of these matters, we must not forget why we are asking the questions: because *Aseneth* is a piece that has lived on, against all odds. In our mind's eye we can see her reaching out in earnestness (and humour?) to a generation much-consumed by method and multiple possibilities: 'Oh, please, why don't you just read me? Maybe the aestheticians are right: you don't absolutely need my pedigree to find me congenial, or to appreciate me. After all, I'm a fiction with a difference. I've proven my staying power, I've lived through many cultures, and many different recensions: I'm not only educational, I'm devotional. Or, just take me for the sheer fun of it.' Midst the application and arguments over method, surrounded by numerous possibilities in reading, students of *Aseneth* will not want to inflict upon this text a process of disintegration. They will want it to continue to speak, or rather to be heard. In the end, it is a book like *Aseneth* that reminds us, if we will allow it, not to take ourselves so seriously.

Further Reading

Humphrey, Edith M., 'On Bees and Best Guesses: The Problem of *Sitz im Leben* from Internal Evidence, as Illustrated by *Joseph and Aseneth*', *Currents in Research: Biblical Studies* 7 (1999), pp. 223-36.

Kraemer, Ross S., *When Aseneth Met Joseph: A Late Antique Tale of the Biblical Patriarch and his Egyptian Wife, Reconsidered* (New York: Oxford University Press, 1998).

INDEXES

INDEX OF REFERENCES

BIBLE

INDEX OF AUTHORS

Guides to the Apocrypha and Pseudepigrapha